Local Authority Support for Sport

A Management Handbook

LONDON: HMSO

1626117

Table of Contents

APPENDICES

Foreword

This management handbook is a companion to a shorter report, *Sport for Whom? – Clarifying the Local Authority Role in Sport and Recreation*, which discussed local authorities' involvement with sport*. That report was aimed primarily at those with responsibility for strategic issues – leaders of councils, committee chairmen, chief executives and chief officers. It covered the challenges facing local authority sport and explored issues such as how to identify the sporting needs of the community, how best to meet those needs within financial constraints, how to set prices and subsidies and how best to help targeted and disadvantaged groups.

This management handbook is aimed primarily at officers and members responsible for preparing an authority for the extension of compulsory competitive tendering to the management of sport and recreation facilities. It is recommended that *Sport for Whom? – Clarifying the Local Authority Role in Sport and Recreation* is read first.

---

* *Throughout this handbook 'sport' is used as a shorthand. It encompasses broader recreational provision which takes place in sports facilities - such as non-sporting events in multi–purpose halls - and the support services, such as bar and catering operations found in sports facilities. Expenditure figures quoted in this handbook take account of such activities.*

Summary

Local authorities have traditionally been major providers and operators of sports facilities, although they are under no statutory obligation to be so. They now manage over 1700 indoor centres, largely built in the last 20 years, as well as many outdoor pitches and golf courses.

Local authorities have nearly always employed their own staff to manage their sports facilities, but in future they will be able to do so for many facilities only when they have won the work in open competition. The provisions of the Local Government Act 1988 have been extended to the management of sports and recreation facilities (with certain exceptions such as many dual use centres, which combine education and public provision). In England, authorities wishing to consider their own direct service organisations for the work will have to put 35% of work to competitive tender in time for contracts to commence by January 1992, 70 per cent by August of that year and all facilities by January 1993. In Wales, implementation is to be phased.

Compulsory competitive tendering is not privatisation. Authorities will still be able to control the way in which facilities are used – opening hours, programme of activities and the prices charged.

Meeting the competitive tendering requirements will require effort and the time available is not great. The experience of the relatively few authorities which have voluntarily put the management of sports facilities out to contract has shown that there are a number of pitfalls to be avoided. However, the evidence suggests that compulsory competition should help authorities provide more efficient services better tailored to local needs.

As they approach their competitive tendering deadline, local authorities should:

— decide their attitude to an in-house bid. The Commission regards the existence of efficient direct service organisations (DSOs) as a beneficial influence on the competitiveness of the market. However, if an authority does not intend to allow a bid by a DSO it is not obliged to follow the full rigour of the Local Government Act 1988. Management buy-outs may appeal to many authorities, but again there are pitfalls;

— reorganise, where necessary, to identify clearly the client and contractor parts of the organisation, both at officer and member level;

— undertake a thorough review of their strategy towards support for sport – what facilities and activities to provide, for whom and at what price;

— decide on contract strategy; whether to use the voluntary sector to manage some facilities, how many contracts to use and whether to include cleaning, catering and ground maintenance in sports management contracts or to let separate contracts for these activities;

— prepare the contract specification. Responsibility for maintaining service quality and setting prices remains with authorities, emphasising the need for clear contract specifications which accurately reflect the authority's policies, particularly on programming and prices. Decisions are required about payment to the contractor. Many contracts will encourage the contractor to maximise the number of users, within the authority's policy constraints. Authorities should avoid arrangements under which they bear losses if the contractor's performance is poorer than expected;

— draw up short lists, evaluate tenders, start up and then manage and supervise the contract. Many evaluations will require the authority to assess tenderer's usage and income forecasts as well as cost predictions;

— improve the efficiency of the recreation DSO, if it is decided to make an in-house bid. Experience from other services suggests that DSOs may need to achieve the performance of the best 10% of in-house operations for them to stand a chance of success if the private sector chooses to bid. Major changes in attitudes, style and conditions of service will often be needed.

Introduction

1. Local authorities in England and Wales have traditionally been major providers and operators of sports facilities. They currently spend about £400 million a year in revenue support, predominantly in subsidising facilities which they themselves provide and operate (Exhibit 1). This is separate from expenditure under Local Education Authority duties and powers, which is not covered in this report. In addition many parks and open spaces contain sports pitches, the cost of which is often not charged to sport; the expenditure on these has been estimated by the Henley Centre For Forecasting as 40% of the expenditure on urban parks and open spaces, a figure which equates to £150m per annum*. Most of this expenditure charged to support for sport is incurred by shire districts, London boroughs and metropolitan districts. County councils do not usually provide public facilities, though some co-operate with district councils to provide dual use facilities; the district council normally meets the notional cost of the public use. There are similar arrangements involving co-operation between education and recreation committees in many metropolitan areas and in London. Some parish councils also provide facilities as do other public bodies such as the Lee Valley Regional Park Authority.

Exhibit 1
NET REVENUE EXPENDITURE ON SPORT
Expenditure has risen in the 1980s

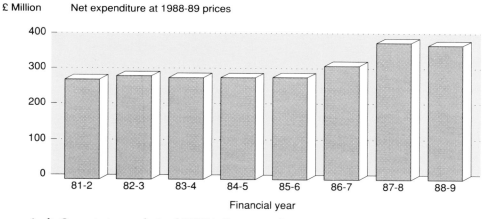

£ Million   Net expenditure at 1988-89 prices

Financial year

Source: Audit Commission analysis of CIPFA 'Leisure and recreation estimates'

2. There is no statutory duty to support sport - expenditure is under the discretionary powers contained in S19 of the Local Government (Miscellaneous Provisions) Act 1976. Local authorities are choosing to be involved. In many cases their reasons are social. In other cases provision may also be linked to economic development and tourism; new facilities make a town or city more attractive to developers, commerce and industry. Whatever the objectives, they have to be pursued within financial constraints (Exhibit 2 overleaf).

---

* *See 'The Economic Impact and Importance of Sport in the United Kingdom', Sports Council, 1986*

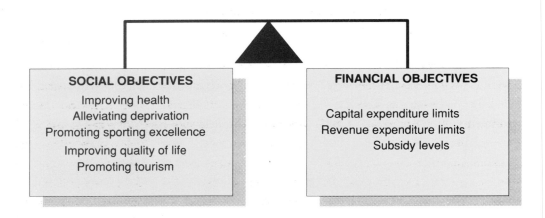

SOCIAL OBJECTIVES	FINANCIAL OBJECTIVES
Improving health Alleviating deprivation Promoting sporting excellence Improving quality of life Promoting tourism	Capital expenditure limits Revenue expenditure limits Subsidy levels

3.   The Commission's research shows that many authorities are confused about their objectives in this area and would do well to reappraise their involvement with sport. These issues are covered in the companion report, which also describes the challenges facing local authorities' sport provision.

4.   This handbook concentrates on one of those challenges – the extension of compulsory competitive tendering (CCT) under the Local Government Act 1988 to the management of many local authority sports facilities. The defined activity 'managing sports and leisure facilities' covers not just pools, squash courts, badminton courts, golf courses and so on but also, for example, centres for boating or water sports, courses for horse racing and centres for flying, ballooning or parachuting. Under CCT, local authorities will be able to use their own workforces (their recreation DSOs) to manage sports facilities only when they have won the work in competition.

5.   De minimis rules will apply and there will be exemption for facilities wholly or partly provided under LEA powers and used exclusively by educational institutions for substantial periods (i.e. many dual use facilities). Otherwise, authorities in England are expected to have to submit to competition the management of facilities equating to 35 per cent of the previous year's gross expenditure in time for contracts to commence by January 1992, 70 per cent by August 1992 and 100 per cent by January 1993. Implementation in Wales is to be phased. Contracts will run for between four and six years.

6.   This report therefore concentrates on the changes needed to respond to CCT and on how the principles behind those changes can also be applied to the operation and management of sports facilities not covered by the legislation. The first chapter discusses decisions about the future of the recreation DSO, management buy-outs and associated companies, the organisational changes needed to identify and separate the client and the contractor roles, the policy review needed before contract specifications are drawn up and the client's budget control role.

7. Chapter 2 describes the competitive tendering process – contract strategy, specification, short list and tender evaluation, contract start up, supervision and management and performance and policy review. Chapter 3 describes what has to be done to prepare the DSO for competition

– the need for improvements, marketing, then staffing issues, control of overheads and other costs, delegated managerial and financial control, the management information needed by the DSO, its business plan and the need for a 'dry run' – a quasi-contractual relationship with the client – in advance of CCT. Chapter 4 discusses dual use operations.

*　　*　　*

8. The report is based on work by a team from the Commission's Directorate of Local Government Studies under the overall direction of Stephen Evans and led by John Gaughan. It included two consultants who had previously been chief officers in local authorities' leisure departments, Wilf Archer and L.S. Whitworth. The fieldwork involved visits to the local authorities listed at Appendix A. The team has received helpful advice from a consultative group containing representatives of the ADC, ACC, AMA, ALA, LBA and of the Sports Council. The team has also consulted the DOE, the Welsh Office, the Sports Council for Wales, other local authority bodies, representatives of companies already managing local authority facilities under contract and professional and trades union bodies during the study. The Commission is grateful to all these bodies for the help and advice they have given. But as with all its reports responsibility for the interpretation of data and for conclusions and recommendations rests with the Commission alone.

9. The Commission's auditors will be following up this report, examining managerial arrangements, preparation for CCT and the efficiency of the recreation DSO in individual authorities in 1990.

1. Setting the Framework

10. Compulsory competitive tendering is not privatisation. Authorities will still retain their powers under Section 19 of the Local Government (Miscellaneous Provisions) Act 1976 and be able to control the way in which facilities are used (opening hours, programme of activities) and the prices charged. As the client in the contractual relationship they will also be able to set quality standards. Default systems and, ultimately, early termination can be used if a contractor fails to meet obligations.

11. Authorities need to decide whether they wish their DSOs to compete for work, and their attitude to possible offers of management buy-outs or the setting up of associated companies. Management buy-out proposals are likely to be a significant feature in sports services.

12. An authority which wishes to retain a DSO will need to ensure that there is a clean split between the client and contractor roles. Although many authorities have separated client and contractor roles in services already affected by CCT, most have not made the separation in the sports and recreation area. The contract specification can be drawn up only after policies on provision, programming and pricing have been settled, and this is best done by carrying out a strategy review, which should be repeated at least every five years. An outline budget must also be set. These preparation steps are described below.

THE FUTURE OF THE DSO

13. A key decision is whether or not the authority wishes to give its own workforce an opportunity to bid. If it chooses not to do so and to rely solely on private contractors, or the voluntary sector, then it may organise contract processes without complying with the CCT requirements of the Local Government Act 1988. This offers a greater choice of contract length and the opportunity to seek management proposals from the private sector, rather than requiring contractors to bid against a predetermined specification. A further attraction is that sporting needs and fashions change rapidly; even a well thought out contract may not remain valid for the four to six year periods required under CCT and may need to be changed. Specifications should be drawn up in a way which will accommodate amendments. Countering the attractions is the experience that the existence of efficient DSOs has a beneficial influence on the competitiveness of the marketplace. Authorities which will not be making a DSO bid should ensure that several contractors tender for the work otherwise they can have no reassurance that prices are as keen as they might be.

14. Many authorities which are now using contractors have not made an in-house bid. However, many authorities will want to allow their own DSO to bid for work. Having made this decision, there are important policy questions, for example, whether the DSO is to be encouraged to bid for all the authority's contracts or only some.

15. The choice can be influenced by the authority's assessment of the DSO's competitiveness. It will be particularly important in authorities which provide riding centres,

artificial ski slopes and other less common facilities. Where several recreation management contracts are won, poor performance on one could drive the account into loss, even though other contracts are profitable. The Secretary of State has the power to close the DSO if its revenue account shows a loss.

16. An authority whose DSO does not bid for some contracts will be in a difficult position if it receives either no tenders from elsewhere for that work or receives only very high bids. The authority may prefer to see the DSO as a contractor of last resort and require it to tender for all contracts but with the expectation that it is unlikely to award some of that work to the DSO.

17. Other factors influencing an authority's attitude towards its DSO may include the authority's desire to operate as a good practice employer; concern about the council's ability to maintain quality of service if private contractors are used; doubts as to whether the private sector will bid; the belief that a strong in-house bid will guarantee a good price, irrespective of who wins the work; the attitude of the DSO itself – whether its employees are prepared to accept change and to work for an operation which has to secure its future in a competitive marketplace.

MANAGEMENT BUY-OUTS

18. Management buy-outs (MBOs) may appeal to many authorities and have already taken place at, for example, Rochford, Hinckley and Bosworth and Westminster. MBOs free existing management from the authority's procedural constraints and from local authority terms and conditions of employment; ownership gives an extra incentive to perform well; current managers may have the incentive to offer a more cost effective service. MBOs also allow the authority to use a contractor which it knows and trusts, and which has a good understanding of its requirements. Some authorities will feel that this is particularly important given that there are few existing sports management contractors in the UK and that they may receive either no bids or only bids from unproven companies. But there are potential difficulties. In particular, an authority will wish to satisfy itself that the negotiation with the MBO is, and is seen to be, fair and impartial.

19. The procedures that should be followed in negotiating a buy-out are presented in the Commission's Management Paper No 6*. The Commission's view is that an authority's fiduciary duty to its ratepayers requires that management buy-out tenders should be tested against the market to ensure keen prices and value for money. This might be done by asking the MBO team to bid against other tenderers for a contract offered by the authority. It may, however, not always be possible to get an MBO off the ground unless the company is guaranteed some initial work.

20. Authorities which do award work to an MBO without competition should be able to demonstrate that this in the interest of their ratepayers/chargepayers and the contract should be for a limited period of, say, one or two years. After the end of the contract period the authority should go through a competitive tendering procedure. If an authority does not wish to award a contract for such a short period it should be able to demonstrate that the proposed contract represents value for money. It is difficult to see how an authority can discharge its fiduciary duty by awarding a contract in excess of the maximum duration laid down in the CCT Statutory Instruments as it would not be regularly testing prices in the market.

---

* *Management Buy-Outs: Public Interest or Private Gain? HMSO, 1990, price £3.50.*

21. Failure to take such precautions could result in considerable windfall profits accruing to a small number of individuals if an uncontested buy-out company wins a long term, over-priced contract. Even if those involved in the MBO have not recognised the full scope for improvements, another operator may spot the potential and buy the MBO company.

22. Authorities also need to ensure that:

— there is no conflict of interest. Officers and employees who are proposing an MBO should declare their intent as soon as the MBO looks feasible. Officers involved in the MBO should not be involved in preparing the contract and must not be involved in short listing and tender evaluation. Likewise the same individuals should not prepare both an MBO and a DSO bid and care is needed to ensure no leakage of information between the two;

— they do not bear the cost of the MBO bid preparation, including senior managers' time spent seeking commercial and financial advice, preparing their bid and negotiating with the authority;

— they take full account of redundancy costs when evaluating MBOs;

— any transfer of assets is at current market value. Independent outside valuation should be obtained.

23. The Local Government and Housing Act 1989 introduces several categories of company in which a local authority has an interest. It is unlikely that an MBO will fall into any of these categories, unless for example, current or previous members or currently serving officers have voting rights in the company. However, the Secretary of State may widen the definition of the categories in a way which may bring in some MBOs. Authorities should take advice as to whether a proposed MBO is affected by the Act.

COMPANIES CONNECTED WITH THE AUTHORITY

24. Some councils may be interested in awarding a contract to a company wholly or partly owned by the authority. The authority may believe that it can then use a contractor it knows and trusts and that it has greater freedom of choice of contract period (provided that no competing DSO bid is made) and in negotiating changes to the contract. Ownership, or retention of a golden share, by the authority offers a guarantee against take-overs by a third party which is not known to the authority. The authority might also seek bids later and sell off the company whose management might then make an offer; the fact that a going concern company was being offered might attract outside interest giving the authority a keen price. There is, however, doubt about local authorities' general powers to establish or participate in an MBO company. Authorities which have an interest in a company need to satisfy themselves that they have the necessary legal power. Insofar as such powers exist, in appropriate circumstances their exercise will have to comply with regulations made by the Secretary of State, under the Local Government and Housing Act 1989. The new capital controls system takes account of such companies' capital funding arrangements. In addition, section 33 of the Local Government Act 1988 requires that an authority shall not enter into a contract for a defined activity with a company with which it is associated without taking reasonable steps to secure competition. (An associated company is defined in Section 33 of the Local Government Act 1988 and Schedule 11 of the Local Government and Housing Act 1989).

25. Authorities which have an interest in a company and wish to award it work should obtain quotes against a written specification, preferably after advertising for tenderers in the way required by the 1988 Act; failing to invite quotes may be unlawful. Where companies are only partly owned by the authority, care is needed to ensure that other parties do not make windfall profits at the authority's expense. The council should not unwittingly bear the full cost of setting up the company and should ensure that any assets are transferred at full, going concern value.

THE CLIENT-CONTRACTOR SPLIT

26. Many councils will wish their DSO to bid for work. If they intend to have a DSO, they need to establish a clear distinction between the authority's client and contractor roles.

27. The client's responsibilities include:

— identifying needs;

— setting usage and participation targets;

— setting price and subsidy levels;

— letting contracts and managing and supervising them;

— monitoring performance to check whether policy objectives are being met.

28. Although many authorities have separated client and contractor roles in activities already affected by competitive tendering, most have not made the separation in the sports and recreation area. Usually the recreation or leisure committee sets policy as well as fixing staffing levels in sports centres. The same senior officers handle client and contractor duties – for example the setting of price levels and the supervision of operational staff.

29. The Commission strongly supports a clear separation of the roles of both members and officers; member separation at committee or board level is recommended. At officer level, separation can best be achieved through separate departments, or, if this is not practicable, as may be the case in some small authorities, through clear definition of roles within departments. The reasoning behind this is more fully explained in Appendix B and the options summarised in Exhibit 3.

Exhibit 3
OPTIONS FOR THE CLIENT – CONTRACTOR SPLIT
Some arrangements are not acceptable

	UNACCEPTABLE	UNDESIRABLE	POSSIBLE	IDEAL
MEMBERS	Same committee	Same committee	Same committee but with separate client and DSO sub-committees	Client committee DSO board
OFFICERS	Same officers	Different officers in same department	Client department Stand alone or umbrella DSO	Client department Stand alone or umbrella DSO

THE CLIENT ROLE

30. In some authorities responsibilities for sport and recreation are fragmented (for example indoor sport may be dealt with by a leisure department and outdoor sport by the parks department). Others have multi-functional leisure departments which may deal with all sport, parks and support for arts groups, municipal theatres, museums and art galleries, tourism and even, in metropolitan and London authorities, libraries. Others have a multiplicity of chief officers dealing with these functions. In some smaller authorities sport and recreation come under the Chief Technical Officer.

31. The main options on the client side are that the client committee and chief officer deal only with recreational activities going to competition, or deal with these and other leisure activities. The choice will be influenced by the size of the authority, the range of sports and other leisure services, by the approach it takes to CCT and by its attitude towards support for the disadvantaged.

32. The first option of the client committee and chief officer dealing only with recreation activities going to competition may not be viable in most authorities; the client function will be too small to justify a chief officer. Authorities will also need to ensure that the number of chief officers does not become excessive, again suggesting that the second option should be chosen, reorganising to reduce the number of chief officers with client leisure responsibilities if necessary. This is, in effect, the position at Surrey Heath where the officer supervising the contractors managing the Arena Centre also acts as client for parks and open spaces and is responsible for the Civic Theatre and the authority's museum.

33. Marketing and promotion of the facility is covered by CCT. But marketing involves not only promotional work to persuade people to use a product or service but deciding what to sell, to whom to sell it and what to charge. Authorities, via their ability to control pricing and programming, will continue to play a major part in marketing. Though contractors will be a major source of ideas, authorities which retain tight programming control will have a particular need for the staff and skills to identify and analyse changing requirements. They may need to buy in, or recruit, marketing expertise or to train existing staff.

34. Managing special arrangements for the disadvantaged and targeted groups – such as devising and promoting passport to leisure schemes and running outreach and sports development programmes – will not always need to be included in contracts let under CCT. Management of sports facilities on premises not predominantly used for sport or physical recreation is, for example, exempt and much sports development work often takes place away from sports centres, in church halls or community centres. Many authorities will want to continue to deal directly with sports development rather than include it in contracts. Such schemes will be a major influence on client staffing and skills, and thus on the organisational arrangements chosen. Marketing expertise will again be important.

35. Under many contracts the client will not only pay the contractor but will be responsible for meeting residual financing costs, the costs of buildings' external maintenance and future capital costs such as those of replacing fixed plant and equipment. Staff are needed to meet these responsibilities; in small authorities specialist support required only occasionally may have to be bought in or shared with other authorities. To illustrate the continuing costs to the client-side

from contracted out management, Surrey Heath's total expenditure on the Arena Centre has increased in real terms since its opening in 1984. As well as contract management fees and debt costs, the authority has spent money on consultancy support for contract supervision and sensibly started to make provision for future repairs. Such expenditure can be considerable and needs to be positively managed.

THE CONTRACTOR ROLE

36. On the contractor side, the recreation DSO could either be included in an umbrella organisation with other statutory DSOs, reporting to their board or committee, or be a free-standing DSO reporting either to the same board as other DSOs, or to its own board/committee.

37. Multi-functional DSOs have proved popular, particularly in smaller authorities, such as Hertsmere and Shepway, for other functions covered by the 1988 Act – ground maintenance, refuse collection, street cleansing, vehicle maintenance, plus, perhaps the building and highways work covered by the 1980 Act – but may not always be appropriate for sports management. Each of these other CCT activities may employ relatively few people. The supervisor responsible for each may lack the expertise to reorganise and prepare a bid, while a full time manager for each service would be an uneconomic overhead. The umbrella approach allows the sharing of management and other overheads. It also means that, providing the DSO wins some work, there is someone in post, committed to the DSO, who will put together a bid in the second round of competition even if the private sector won a contract the first time around.

38. These other activities do, however, share a common technical services background. Recreation management requires different skills and recreation DSOs in many authorities are likely to contain staff from different backgrounds with a sufficient range of skills to exist as a separate organisation. Chichester District Council's Westgate Leisure Centre is, for example, managed by in-house staff who already have a quasi-contractual relationship with the authority and who are, in effect, a stand alone DSO.

39. A halfway house is possible. Some authorities have found it difficult to decide how to treat their ground maintenance DSO. They fear that it may be too small to be a viable stand-alone body but may also face problems if it is included in an umbrella technical services DSO whose senior management may not understand its problems. Much ground maintenance work is in support of recreation. The recreation DSO and the ground maintenance DSO might therefore share a senior manager, particularly in authorities where client responsibilities for both will be dealt with by the one department or where much of the ground maintenance work is to be included in the sports management contract (invoking S2(5) of the 1988 Act). An alternative is to link two activities involving income generation – sport and catering.

40. The attitude and skills of the senior officers involved are crucial. People do not have to use local authority sports facilities and are normally charged for their use; whoever manages the DSO must be customer oriented and businesslike. The right managerial attitude may be more important than the professional qualifications held.

41. In general, the Commission has found that the best DSOs have lean management structures with only three or four layers from manager to operative.

THE CHOICE

42. Since the final choice on both the client and DSO side must take account of matters such as the size of the authority, its style, the calibre of its existing staff, the current efficiency of its operations and so on, no single solution can be common to all authorities; each authority should review its structure and identify the solution which best suits its requirements. Exhibit 4 summarises factors that should be considered.

Exhibit 4
EVALUATING ORGANISATIONAL STRUCTURES IN SPORTS SERVICES
Authorities should evaluate their organisational structures against a number of criteria

The management structure should:	Yes ✓	No ✗
1. Facilitate the setting of objectives.		
2. Enable clients to obtain adequate overall resources.		
3. Ensure fair competition between the DSO and other tenderers. To do so it must:		
– minimise potential conflicts of interest		
– minimise opportunities for corruption		
– permit accurate costing of DSO work		
– allow DSO managers to manage.		
4. Require lean staffing levels and low overheads.		
5. Be internally consistent; in particular committee and management structures should be aligned.		
6. Provide for clear accountability and allow objective and accurate monitoring of performance on service delivery.		
7. Promote an attitude of adaptability so that services can be altered to suit changing circumstances.		

43. The number of client side staff, the expertise they need, the detailed organisational structure to use and the size of the client budget will be influenced by the policies the authority is following – whether, for example, it is strongly committed to client side operation of passport to leisure schemes and sports development and outreach programmes. One option is initially to create a small client unit which carries out the strategy review described below. Client arrangements can be refined as part of the review.

THE STRATEGY REVIEW

44. Councils need to reappraise their involvement with sport in preparation for CCT. They should do this against the background of an analysis of changing social trends. The first step

should be to define the council's social and financial objectives. This may lead to a reconsideration of the activities it supports and its approach to pricing, subsidy and special arrangements for targeted and disadvantaged groups. It should certainly involve devising and implementing means of measuring effectiveness. Reappraisal should begin now and be complete before contracts are awarded – otherwise it may be more difficult to implement new policies. Authorities which have the necessary in-house expertise may need to buy in help or seek advice from Regional Sports Councils if they cannot divert staff from their normal duties. Smaller authorities may prefer to contract out the whole exercise.

45. The reappraisal should be formalised as a strategy review and repeated at least every five years. The exercise is intended to provide a framework for the authority's complete involvement with sport and should therefore cover matters such as sports outreach and development and the management and role of dual use facilities, exempt from CCT, as well as new provision issues; it should not concentrate solely on facilities affected by CCT. Reviews should be supplemented by smaller annual reappraisals. The review is summarised in Exhibit 5 and questions to be answered summarised in Exhibit 6 (overleaf). Objectives need to be defined and a range of options for meeting need considered and costed. Targets should be set both in social and financial terms and the information needed to monitor the extent to which they are being met should be identified.

DECIDING ON SOCIAL OBJECTIVES

46. The reasons for local authority involvement with sport are discussed in the companion report *Sport for Whom?*. Authorities should decide what types of need they are trying to meet, distinguishing between the needs of people who would like to take part in sport, or take part more frequently, but are unable to because facilities are not available; of people who have not expressed a need but will use facilities with relatively little prompting, and of those people with no interest in sport who will not take part automatically if facilities become available. Helping this last group may be costly. Decisions should take account of the needs of minority and other groups, including disabled people. *Compulsory competitive tendering - policy guidelines for leisure managers* issued by the British Sports Association for the Disabled discusses policy and other CCT issues affecting disabled people. Policy on support for excellence should also be examined.

ASSESSING NEED

47. Sports participation is supply led, i.e. depends on the availability of facilities. The authority should first identify the facilities serving its area, whether public, voluntary or private sector and the activities offered. Existing and planned provision in adjacent authorities should also be examined; catchment areas are not defined by local government boundaries. The exercise may involve work with maps, local directories, enquiries of local schools and other educational establishments providing dual use facilities, local companies, youth clubs, voluntary bodies, sports clubs and leagues. Computerised database information on facilities is available in some parts of the country, for example in London from Online Leisure Information. The results can be used to set up an inventory of local facilities.

Exhibit 5

THE STRATEGY REVIEW

The strategy review involves the following

Decide the authority's social objectives. What types of need is it trying to meet?	Identify current and future needs	Identify the financial constraints the authority has to work within - revenue - capital	Set targets and decide how to meet needs	Identify client side staffing needs (numbers, skills and structure) and budgets	Identify the management information needed to monitor progress
• access • participation • needs of keen sports men and women • suppressed demand from other people • needs of people with no current interest in sport	• numbers of people who don't now participate • areas without ready access to facilities • demographic change • changes in fashion • changes in expectation	• new capital controls • community charge	• participation rates • accessibility • usage of local authority facilities • subsidy levels	• policy review and monitoring • contractor supervision and monitoring • passports to leisure • sports development and outreach	• participation measures • expenditure measures • responsibilities for collection and monitoring • staff • budgets

15

Exhibit 6

QUESTIONS FOR THE LEISURE STRATEGY REVIEW

All authorities should ask themselves these questions

Questions	Considerations
What sports related services do we currently provide? Who does and doesn't use them, and why?	• user surveys • contact with clubs, leagues etc. • surveys among people who don't use the services
Who else is providing services to our community and what are those services?	• provision by adjacent authorities, voluntary and private sectors
What are we trying to achieve and who are we trying to help?	• accessibility orientation (attention concentrates on location of facilities, no price barriers to use by the poor) or • participation orientation (actively seeking to increase participation)
What needs are we trying to meet?	• expressed needs • suppressed demand or • needs as determined by the authority (paternalistic approach)
What constraints are we working under?	• legal (e.g. CCT) • financial (capital, revenue)
How will needs change?	• demography • fashion
What will we do as they change?	• respond to trends or be innovative • support a wide range of activities or concentrate on a selected few (a 'core curriculum')
What should we leave to the private or voluntary sectors?	• activities • facilities
How can we best meet needs?	• what to provide • which activities to support • pricing and subsidy policy • special arrangements for target groups
What resources are required?	• budgets (capital and revenue) • staff (numbers, skills, training needs)
How do we monitor what we are achieving?	• management information needs
What do we need to do to implement our ideas?	• organisational change • assignment of responsibilities

48. Next, the authority should identify facilities which are not currently used for sport by the general public, but have the potential for such use. Examples include community halls, church halls and facilities in schools, colleges, universities and polytechnics and facilities used by HM Forces. The cost implications of bringing them into use also need to be identified.

49. The authority should then check who uses the existing facilities. Consultants and marketing firms can be used to carry out surveys to obtain information on users. Students on business courses at local colleges may also be used to carry out the work, though their lack of experience may mean that careful supervision is needed to ensure that questionnaires are well structured, and that interview techniques are adequate. The exercise need not be elaborate. The Office of Population Censuses and Surveys, Sports Councils and other bodies have published a considerable amount of information on sports participation. Survey work may need to do no more than confirm that the pattern in a particular authority, adjusted for its local demographic and social structure, is in line with the national pattern. Computer breakdowns of data on local demography such as ACORN analyses are readily available.

50. Clubs, voluntary bodies and leagues can be contacted to obtain information on their membership. Local schools and other education establishments can be approached to find out about students' involvement with sport, both during the day and as an extra-curricular activity. Private sector operators can also be approached, though here commercial confidentiality may limit the information made available. People and organisations including those representing the unemployed, ethnic minorities, disabled people and other target groups contacted during surveys can also be asked for views on the quality of existing facilities, on the range of activities offered, and on whether there are gaps in provision.

51. This information can be used to identify groups in the community which are under-represented among sports participants, activities not catered for and parts of the authority without access to facilities. Local transport and communications arrangements need to be considered here. Many people are unwilling to spend much time travelling to facilities and, for most sports, most users spend 20 minutes or less getting to a facility. Car owners will want easy parking; people without cars need facilities close to homes or workplaces or which are well served by public transport. Access can be a particular problem for small rural communities. Further work can be carried out to confirm findings – for example contact with community groups in areas lacking provision, contact with groups representing sections of society under-represented among current participants and contact with individual local schools to check how their requirements are likely to change in response to local financial management and the introduction of the national curriculum.

52. This snapshot view is not, however, sufficient. Fashions in sport and leisure are volatile. The age structure of society is also changing (Exhibit 7 overleaf) with a decline in the numbers of young people, who are major users of current facilities. This may influence the mix of provision needed; older people may be more interested in golf than squash, for example. Authorities therefore need to take account of projected demographic change. Planning departments can offer advice.

53. The process can take account of national recommendations on provision levels issued by the Sports Council and other bodies. Recommendations have, however, usually been couched

Exhibit 7
**PROJECTED CHANGES IN THE AGE STRUCTURE OF SOCIETY IN ENGLAND
AND WALES 1985-95**
There will be a decline in the number of teenagers and young adults, who are major users of sports facilities

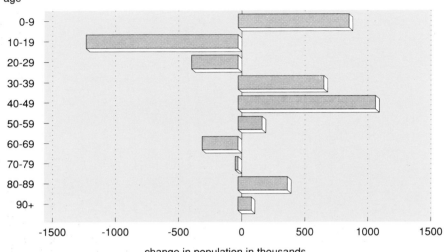

Source: Data from 'Annual abstract of statistics 1988'

in broad terms – area, or number, of facilities per head of population. More complex models such as one developed for the Scottish Sports Council are becoming available. They can help identify gaps in existing provision, although they are based on historic usage and participation patterns and therefore unable to predict the effects of changes in fashion or expectation. The overall process is summarised in Exhibit 8.

54. Survey and other work of this sort can not only help identify the needs of the community but can later be drawn upon to help decide the role which the authority's own facilities are to play in meeting those needs. Bolton's approach to provision has been strongly influenced by work of this sort. Chelmsford (Case Study 1) and Lliw Valley have also carried out reviews.

IDENTIFYING FINANCIAL OBJECTIVES AND CONSTRAINTS

55. The authority's financial objectives and constraints should be examined, as discussed in *Sport for whom?*. Capital constraints should be identified to help not only with decisions with new provision but with decisions on re-investment in, or upgrades to, existing facilities. In addition plant and fixed equipment, particularly in buildings opened in the early to mid-1970s, may be reaching the end of its life and may need to be replaced while CCT contracts are in operation. The arrangements to apply during such replacement should be clearly set out in contracts; an understanding of the capital constraints affecting replacement is an essential prerequisite.

Exhibit 8

ASSESSING NEED

Assessing need is the cornerstone of the strategy review

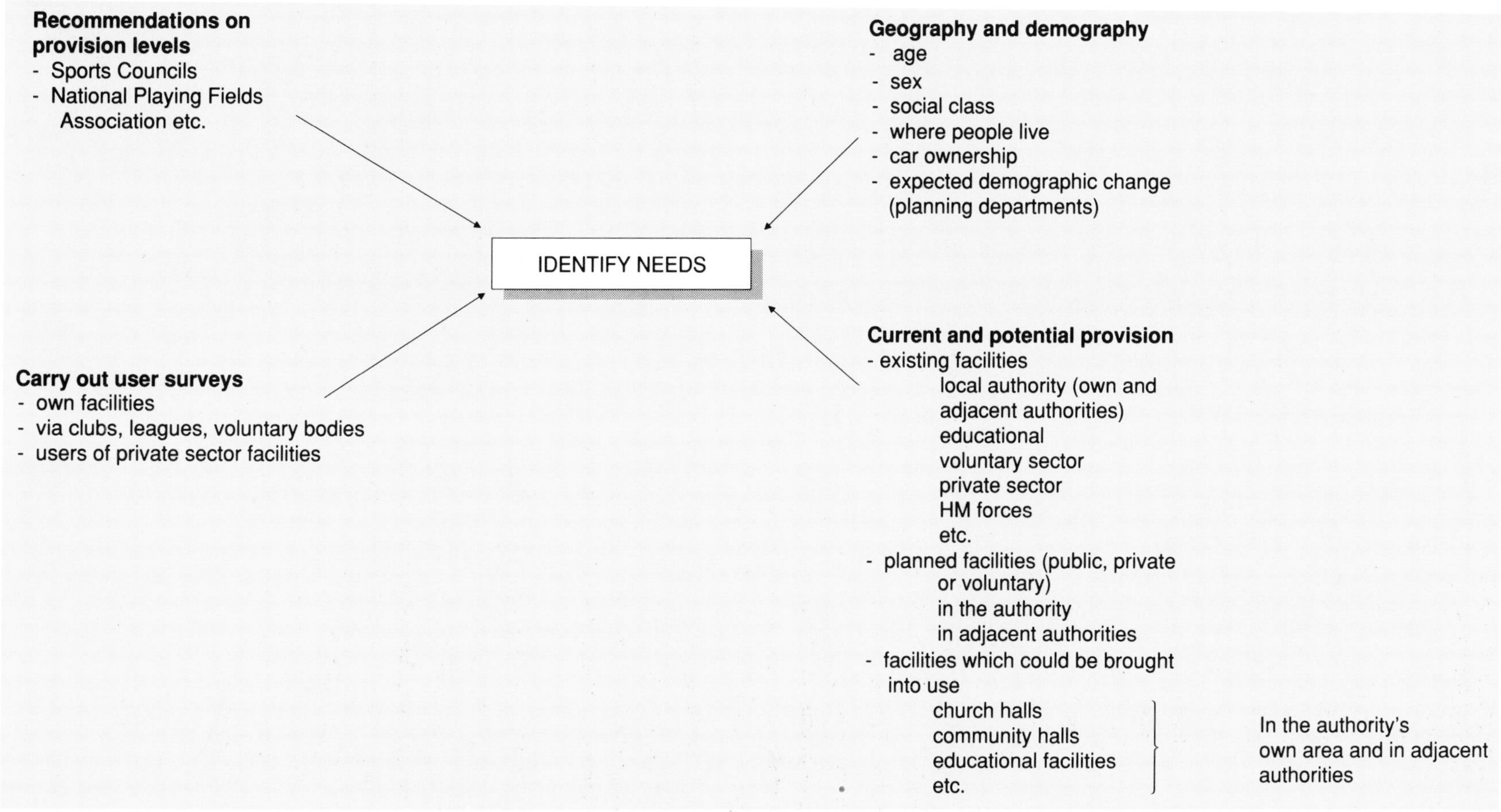

Recommendations on provision levels
- Sports Councils
- National Playing Fields Association etc.

Geography and demography
- age
- sex
- social class
- where people live
- car ownership
- expected demographic change (planning departments)

Current and potential provision
- existing facilities
  local authority (own and
  adjacent authorities)
  educational
  voluntary sector
  private sector
  HM forces
  etc.
- planned facilities (public, private
  or voluntary)
  in the authority
  in adjacent authorities
- facilities which could be brought
  into use
  church halls
  community halls   In the authority's
  educational facilities   own area and in adjacent
  etc.   authorities

IDENTIFY NEEDS

Carry out user surveys
- own facilities
- via clubs, leagues, voluntary bodies
- users of private sector facilities

Case Study 1 : LEISURE STRATEGY REVIEW

Authority: Chelmsford Borough Council

Chelmsford carried out a review of recreational facilities in 1974 which established a borough-wide position statement on existing facilities; identified areas of shortfall and enabled the council to consider recreational development for the future. Population has grown since then and new needs might exist.

A further review was carried out in 1987. Questionnaires were distributed to a wide range of local organisations – Essex County Council (a major provider via its educational establishments), parish councils, churches, youth clubs, other voluntary bodies, community centres, private sector sports and social clubs, private sector health clubs, sports clubs and associations, riding schools, football leagues, the South Woodham Ferrers Sports Council, Chelmsford District Sports Council and Eastern Region Sports Council – to help assess provision and need.

Information was compared with existing records and a database on facilities throughout the Borough established. Follow-up contact was made with questionnaire respondents to assess views on demand.

Areas where existing facilities and demand did not match were then identified, using standards and advice from the Sports Council, the National Playing Fields Association and other bodies.

Short, medium and long term plans were drawn up. Those with capital implications have been fed into the Council's capital programme.

The work suggested that most indoor needs were being met but that a requirement for a new pool at South Woodham Ferrers should be evaluated in more detail.

Requirements for parkland and children's play areas were identified as was the need to examine provision of artificial pitches, and a need for improved athletics facilities.

56. Revenue constraints should also be considered – in particular any pressure to reduce subsidies, and increase prices, arising from the introduction of the community charge. For example, contractors and not the authority may receive the benefit if price increases are introduced after contracts have begun.

57. In other services subject to CCT there have been significant efficiency improvements often leading to reductions in unit costs of 20 per cent or more. The limited experience of contracted out operations in sport and recreation suggests that improvements in efficiency are again likely, and will probably result in both a decreased cost to the authority and an increased number of users per facility. This is because many contracts will encourage the contractor not only to pay attention to costs but to maximise income within the authority's policy constraints, and hence to increase the number of users.

SETTING TARGETS

58. Sports management involves responding to a changing market. It is not, therefore, an exact science. Authorities can nevertheless set achievable targets both in social terms – for example 35% of men aged between 40 and 50 to take part in sport at least once a week; everyone

in the authority to live within 30 minutes travelling time of an indoor pool – and financial ones – for example a maximum subsidy per user visit to the authority's facilities. Achievement can then be measured against targets to help discover whether social objectives are being met and to help relate cost to achievement. Targets should be set both for the overall achievement of social policies (e.g. target participation levels, irrespective of whether or not this involves use of the authority's facilities) and specifically for the authority's own facilities (e.g. target usage levels).

MEETING NEED

59. Options for meeting need (Exhibit 9) include new provision by the authority or reinvestment in its existing facilities, changes in the mix of activities offered by its existing facilities, the approach to prices and subsidies at its facilities, and measures such as passport to leisure schemes and sports development work to stimulate participation by targeted and disadvantaged groups.

Exhibit 9
MEETING NEED
A range of issues should be considered in meeting needs, and provision of new facilities is not necessarily the main one

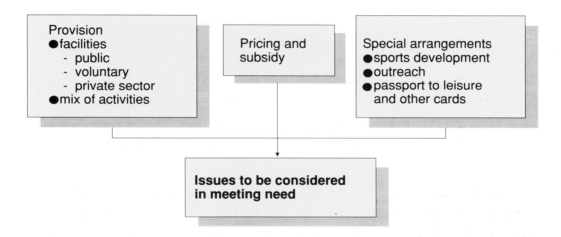

PROVISION

60. Attention should not, however, concentrate solely on provision by the authority itself (Exhibit 10 ovearleaf). Cooperation with other authorities or with the private or voluntary sectors may be more effective. Even *direct provision by the authority* involves choices. Investment in indoor facilities may, for example, preclude investment in outdoor provision for some years. There can also be choices in indoor provision. For example, a large town centre facility might be used for competitive county and international events as well as local ones and be important in urban regeneration, but it may preclude investment in outlying areas. Alternatives involving smaller, more local facilities or converting disused buildings such as church halls (or a former territorial army drill hall, as in Bolton) may be preferable, particularly in rural areas. Some social objectives – for example, improving the quality of life or extending the range of leisure opportunities – can also be served by supporting other activities, e.g. theatres and arts groups.

Exhibit 10

PROVISION

There are a number of options for provision, not confined to facilities provided by the local authority

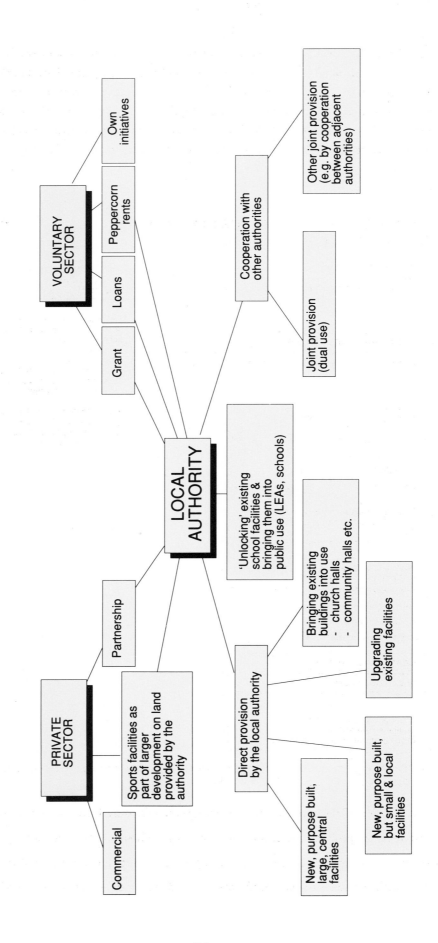

61. Predicting the usage, income and cost of a new sports facility is not easy. Experience in the private sector shows that the demand for new leisure facilities is particularly difficult to assess, making new investment risky. Any need for major new facilities identified during the leisure strategy review should be investigated in more detail using an approach such as that described by the Sports Council (Exhibit 11). Such a detailed examination should take account of potential non-sporting recreational use, which can be important both financially and to the overall service a facility provides.

Exhibit 11
PREPARING TO PROVIDE A MAJOR NEW FACILITY
The Sports Council has suggested the following approach

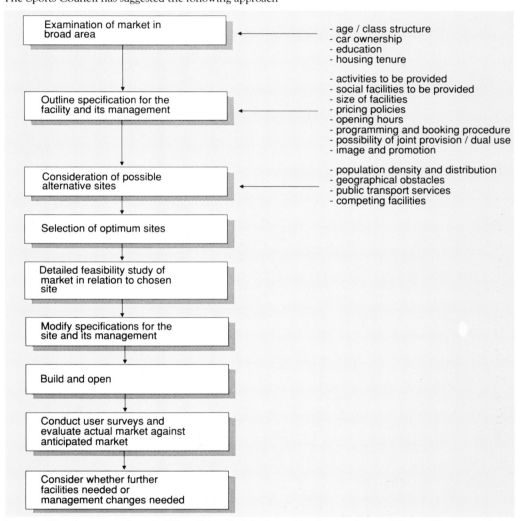

Source: Based on procedures in 'Identifying the Market – Catchment Areas of Sports Centres and Swimming Pools', Sports Council, 1983.

62. The difficulty in estimating the operating costs of new facilities is sometimes exacerbated by weaknesses in project control and building design. Though initial designs may be carefully costed, members may later require major changes, the operating implications of which are not analysed with the same rigour. Authorities should ensure they have professional recreation

management advice when designing new facilities. This might come from consultants, from the DSO or from a management company.

63. *Inter-authority co-operation* is an alternative form of provision and might involve:

a. *Joint provision of dual use facilities.* This can involve a county council, as local education authority and the district council. (Nottinghamshire has particularly well developed joint provision arrangements.) Responsibilities for capital and revenue costs are usually at present based on a percentage allocation of costs between the two parties, but vary from centre to centre depending on the facilities and extent of educational and public use. *Other types of dual use* are possible in which the local education authority, school or other educational establishment makes facilities available for public use without subvention from other authorities or departments. Many educational establishments have facilities which can be, but are not, used in this way. Unlocking them would increase provision without significant additional capital expenditure. Dual use involving cooperation between the education and recreation (or equivalent) committee is also possible in metropolitan districts and London boroughs and is, for example, a major part of Bolton's provision.

b. *Other cooperation between overlapping authorities.* In one authority visited a sports centre was built by the district council on land provided by the town council. The district council manages the centre; the town council provides and runs adjacent outdoor facilities.

c. *Joint provision between adjacent authorities.* Downshire Golf Course is, for example, overseen by a Joint Committee of Bracknell Forest and Wokingham Councils; Gunnersbury Park London, which provides many outdoor sports pitches, is managed by a Joint Committee of Hounslow and Ealing.

64. Other approaches are also possible – provision by developers, and use of grants and loans to help the voluntary sector.

65. *Provision by developers* occurs when a developer finances a facility as part of a bigger scheme on land purchased from the authority. A new sports centre under construction in Bromley is one example of such an arrangement (Case Study 2). The value of the facility is to be treated as part of the capital receipt under the new capital controls system, possibly reducing the attractions of the approach. Project management can also have difficulties from the authority's viewpoint; the developer is providing a facility for the council but has received payment – use of the site – before the work is complete, removing the client's normal control over building work. A centre, once built, can be run by the developer or by the authority. Arrangements which require the developer to manage the centre, without revenue support from the authority can have difficulties; tensions have emerged in one case because of the developer's wish to operate commercially, and the authority's desire to preserve the 'Sport For All' approach written into the original agreement.

66. Another approach is to contribute to the capital costs and possibly, any operating costs incurred by a voluntary organisation. The long-standing arrangement at Harlow is an example. Management is then free of local authority rules and procedures. A fundamental shift in the approach adopted by such an organisation could, however, upset the balance of an authority's sport and recreation strategy. In addition the approach has not been universally successful. Some authorities have taken over control from voluntary organisations which have run into difficulties. Voluntary organisations must be set up by some third party if they are to be eligible for loans or grants under S19(3) of the Local Government (Miscellaneous Provisions) Act 1976.

67. Authorities can also lease facilities to the voluntary sector at *low rents*, again supporting local initiatives without the burden of facility management. Councils using these approaches may wish to ensure access is readily available to the general public and not limited to a small group and make public access a condition of the arrangement.

68. Attention should not focus on new provision alone. The review should also examine the age, likely life and current use of *existing facilities*. Reinvestment requirements should be identified and fed into the capital programme after risks and revenue implications have been examined in the same way as for new facilities. Thamesdown's reinvestment in waterslides at its Oasis Centre is an example of an addition to an existing facility (Case Study 3 overleaf).

69. In some cases catchment populations may have changed so radically, possibly because other facilities have been built since the centre opened, that a facility now appears over-large. In others, renovation and repair may cost more than the authority can afford or is prepared to spend for the benefits being received. Options include closure with disposal of the site or a redevelopment which provides a smaller facility on the site.

ACTIVITIES SUPPORTED

70. The types of activity the authority wishes to support should be identified. The review should not, however, set out detailed programmes; these should be changed as customer requirements alter. Instead it should concentrate on more strategic issues such as the balance the authority wishes to strike between club bookings, school lettings and casual public use. Clear policies are needed before contracts can be let.

OPENING HOURS

71. Opening hours for facilities provided by the authority should be reappraised. Although most councils are anxious to provide good public access and some groups, such as top flight sports men and women and business people, may want early morning sessions, usage is often low on weekday mornings. Shorter, well publicised opening hours may reduce variable costs without deterring use. Different summer and winter opening hours may be used in centres with high usage by holidaymakers, as is already done at Sheringham. Any extra costs of ineffective opening may be locked into place once contracts are let.

SUBSIDIES AND PRICES

72. Many authorities charge low prices and subsidise all users in order to guarantee access for disadvantaged groups. The potential ineffectiveness of this is highlighted in *Sport for whom?*. An untargeted subsidy can benefit a few at the expense of the majority, while increasing prices for those who can afford to pay them does not necessarily deter use. Wherever possible, the highest subsidies should be targeted at particular groups while other users, though still possibly subsidised, are asked to pay more. This promotes social objectives while protecting financial aims. Real increases in prices, possibly phased in over several years so effects on usage can be monitored, offer an opportunity to increase income, particularly if linked to better marketing and to schemes which protect the disadvantaged. Up-to-date survey information on the social backgrounds of people who use the authority's facilities are an important input to decisions on subsidy and price.

73. Charges for schools' sessions at public facilities need to be reappraised. Local budgets for schools required by the Education Reform Act 1988 mean that schools may pay more attention

to the prices they are charged. They may shop around for the best deal, or even abandon sessions if they appear too expensive. The introduction of the national curriculum may also influence schools' use of public facilities. Authorities need a clear policy on the subsidies they are prepared to offer educational establishments. Decisions should bear in mind the role of schools' sessions in introducing people to sport, and thus in meeting social objectives, as well as in helping create future customers.

74. Price changes need to be handled sensitively. Different groups in society tend to be interested in different sports. Prices may be set so that the largest subsidies go to activities of most interest to target groups. Special arrangements may also be needed for children; some charges might be less than 50% of the adult rate, the percentage commonly used now. Different prices might even be charged at different centres, reflecting the different social characteristics of their catchment areas.

75. Major changes in pricing policy and arrangements to support target groups should be implemented before contracts are let to ensure the authority receives the financial benefits.

SPECIAL ARRANGEMENTS
76. The authority should identify any target groups for which it wishes to make special provision and the methods to be used – sports outreach, sports development and passport to leisure type cards whose holders pay reduced charges. Some authorities, particularly those providing regional or sub-regional facilities or facilities aimed at the tourist trade, may make discount cards available to all residents or even have three pricing tiers – visitors, residents, target groups.

IMPLEMENTING THE RECOMMENDATIONS
77. The action needed to implement the recommendations – who will be responsible, the timetable they will work to and the revenue and capital costs – should also be identified. Client side staffing – numbers, skills required, training needed and organisation – and budgets should also be identified.

MEASURING SUCCESS
78. The implementation arrangements should take account of management information requirements. Measuring financial success is relatively straightforward; success in meeting long term social objectives such as better health cannot, however, readily be measured in the short term, and is difficult to relate to individual initiatives. Other social objectives such as quality of life can be evaluated but are influenced by many factors other than sports provision. Authorities can, however, monitor the success of their programmes using participation measures as intermediate indicators of social achievement. Some possible social and financial performance indicators of interest to the client are shown in Appendix C. Though they do not distinguish between client and contractor needs, Pannell Kerr Forster's work for the Audit Inspectorate in 1983* and work by the Greater London and South East Region of the Sports Council[†] both offer detailed advice on performance measures.

---

* *Development and operation of leisure centres (selected case studies)*, HMSO, 1983
† *Measuring Performance, Management Paper No. 1, Sports Council, Greater London and South East Region*, 1988

79. All authorities should identify the procedures needed to measure success. As well as the strategy review, sample surveys of users may be needed from time to time to check who is receiving subsidies and find out users' views on the service provided. These can be complemented by regular management information from centres, possibly provided by operators under the terms of their contract. Sample surveys of local clubs and voluntary bodies may also be needed to give the overall picture. Data can be drawn together in the annual position reappraisal.

*   *   *

80. This chapter has described the changes and preparations needed in response to CCT. The next chapter describes how to prepare and let contracts; though couched in terms of CCT its advice can also be applied to contracts let by authorities which have abandoned the in-house option and decided to rely solely on the private or voluntary sectors, contracts awarded by councils allowing competitive MBOs and by authorities setting up associated companies.

2. The Competitive Tendering Process

81. Once the client and DSO roles have been separated and the policy objectives set, the prime task is to decide how to achieve those objectives – the contract strategy to follow, the specification to use, how to handle short list and tender evaluation, how to supervise and manage contracts and how to monitor performance. The experience available is limited; the Institute of Leisure and Amenity Management (ILAM) and the Institute of Baths and Recreation Management (IBRM) have, however, prepared advice*. Although over 20 centres are already managed under contract, not all of that work has been put to competition and many contracts have been amended as deficiencies and weaknesses became apparent. The special study examined many of the existing contracts and from these, and experience of other services put out to tender, distilled the good practices which are discussed in this chapter.

82. The authority should decide on contract strategy; whether to use the voluntary sector to manage some facilities, how many contracts to use and whether to include cleaning, catering and ground maintenance at sports facilities in management contracts or to let separate contracts. It then needs to prepare the contract specification. In particular, decisions are required about payment to the contractor, programming and pricing. The authority needs to draw up short lists of contractors. Evaluating tenders will often be more involved than in most other services because in many cases it will require the authority to assess tenderers' usage and income forecasts as well as cost predictions. Finally the authority needs to begin and manage and supervise the contract.

CONTRACT STRATEGY
83. Contract strategy involves issues such as whether the DSO is to bid for all the authority's sports management work, the number of contracts to use and the activities to include in contracts.

CIRCUMSTANCES WHERE TENDERING MAY NOT BE APPROPRIATE
84. Even authorities which want their DSO to bid for work should consider whether in-house or contract management is appropriate in all circumstances. There may be problems in finding contractors willing to take on outdoor pitches scattered throughout parks and open spaces, especially if responsibility for bars and catering in pavilions and club houses is excluded, either because there are none, or because separate catering contracts have already been let. Linking the management of outdoor pitches to that of indoor centres will make the latter less attractive, possibly reducing the number of bids and the keenness of prices. Other facilities may have low turnovers, again making them unattractive to contractors.

85. So there are some circumstances in which tendering may not bring significant benefits. In many such instances facilities could be passed to the voluntary sector (bowls clubs, cricket

---
* *Management of sports and leisure facilities*, ILAM/IBRM Longmans 1989

clubs, etc.), which is exempt from CCT. Continuing public use could be written into agreements. Facilities can be leased to voluntary organisations at a peppercorn rent, with the club or association receiving a separate annual grant from the authority. This avoids another potential problem of supervising contractors carrying out ground maintenance of cricket pitches and bowling greens. The effects of poor work may be substantial but may not appear for some time, making it difficult to prove liability. A club should have a strong vested interest in quality and might even take on a groundsman formerly employed by the authority. Since one season of mismanagement can ruin a valuable asset, clubs should be required to demonstrate that they have, or will have, the necessary expertise. Authorities will also want to be sure that the club's commitment does not depend upon the enthusiasm of a handful of members. A possible drawback is that clubs may try and discourage public use and reserve facilities for themselves. Agreements with clubs will need to be as carefully and tightly drawn up as agreements with contractors and will also need to be supervised and managed.

86. Alternatively, responsibility for pitches in parks and open spaces can be a minor duty of a local authority employee primarily engaged in tasks not covered by CCT, e.g. client staff supervising ground maintenance contracts. It need not then go to competition (S2(6) of the Local Government Act 1988).

87. A third option is to include pitch letting in the ground maintenance contract. Enfield has, for example, included tennis court and putting green lettings in its ground specification. This can make sense but it is important to guard against conflicts of interest; a contractor might declare a pitch unplayable in marginal conditions to avoid the cost of repairing damage.

88. Competitive tendering should not be by-passed to protect inefficient in-house staff. The Commission's auditors will review the practices of authorities which seek to avoid competitive tendering, to check that they achieve value for money.

GOLF COURSES
89. Golf courses present particular problems. At present many are used by affiliated clubs which either lease the club house from the authority, or have themselves financed the construction of all or part of the building. Some have several clubs. Mostly, they already use the private sector for catering and bar services, either by agreement between the authority and a contractor or between an affiliated club and a contractor. Usually they possess a course professional, typically self-employed, but under contract to the authority, sometimes receiving a retainer and usually receiving free or low cost use of shop facilities in return for providing shop services, equipment hire and lessons. Many also collect green fees, either under the terms of their contract, or as an ad hoc local arrangement. In addition many authorities have no-one on the client side with green keeping expertise; the dominant technical knowledge can be held by the head of the parks DSO gang maintaining the course. This is already a problem for authorities including golf courses in ground maintenance contracts.

90. In many authorities there are thus few golf course management functions, other than marketing and promotion, that have to be put to tender under the 1988 Act. For example, Bolton has only one, part-time employee at its municipal course.

91. A move to comprehensive management contracts is desirable. The net annual cost of municipal golf courses in England and Wales is only £2 million and many generate an operating profit (Exhibit 12). More may move into operating profit if costs fall, and usage rises, in response to competition. In reality golf courses are more profitable than revealed by local authorities' accounts as these exclude the profit made by existing bar and catering franchisees and professionals' profits; the shop, equipment hire and coaching provide the bulk of professionals' income.

Exhibit 12
GOLF COURSE PROFITABILITY
Profitability varies markedly from course to course

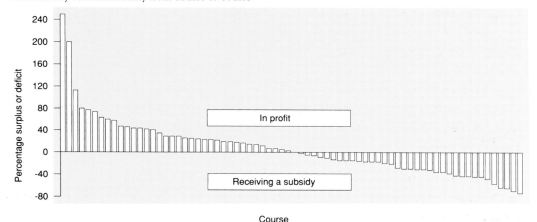

Course

Source: Audit Commission analysis of CIPFA 'Leisure and recreation estimates 1988-89' for authorities with a single 18 hole course

92. Most local authority courses are therefore actual or potential profit earners; authorities can therefore consider franchising the entire operation, under terms which require continued public access. The operator would then pay the authority a fee. Professionals may be interested in such arrangements as may existing private sector operators. Many authorities may therefore operate outside CCT, sometimes offering long contracts to make it more attractive for companies to invest in courses – provide driving ranges, coaching facilities, better clubhouses, bar and catering facilities, family areas, children's play areas and so on.

93. The affiliated club still has a role – for example providing a way for beginners to obtain a handicap – but may not be a good management alternative to contracting out or franchising. Relations between some authorities and clubs have been difficult, with clubs pressing for further benefits for their members – advance bookings, exclusive use of the course on particular days for tournaments etc. – which restrict public use. Objective supervision of some clubs' management of courses might be difficult given the close relationships between some clubs and the local authority; councillors and senior officers are sometimes active club members, creating a potential conflict of interest.

ACTIVITIES INCLUDED IN CONTRACTS

94. Authorities can either let separate contracts for catering, building cleaning and ground maintenance or, where they are provided in conjunction with a sports facility, can incorporate them in the management contract, invoking S2(5) of the 1988 Act.

31

95. *Catering* is important because attractive bars and restaurants help generate repeat business, while profits can be used to offset losses on other parts of the operation. Income can also be generated by special events – social evenings, use of the main hall for wedding receptions and so on. Catering is frequently combined with sports activities to produce a leisure package.

96. Operators and DSOs may therefore prefer to see catering included in the contract rather than awarded separately. One authority is considering buying out its existing catering franchisees so it can offer comprehensive sports management contracts.

97. *Cleaning* is also important; a grubby centre is less likely to generate repeat business. Commercial operators and DSOs may again prefer a contract which gives them direct control, particularly since lifeguards, or other leisure centre staff, now often carry out poolside and other cleaning between swimming sessions as part of their normal duties; specialist cleaners may only be used either after a centre has closed or in the morning before it opens. Separate catering and cleaning contracts should not normally be used. Where they are employed, responsibilities need to be clearly specified, particularly for bars and cafeteria.

98. Control of *grass cutting and other horticultural work* is probably less crucial to commercial operators except in sports requiring high quality turf, such as golf, cricket and bowls.

THE NUMBER OF CONTRACTS

99. The way in which competition is being phased in England may also result in many authorities offering several contracts rather than one contract (though the percentages of work to go to contract by the different dates are likely to be minimum figures and the dates themselves latest dates, allowing authorities to put out more work and go to competition earlier providing they do not behave anti-competitively in so doing and otherwise comply with requirements in the Act).

100. The number of contracts is also likely to vary with the size of the authority. Irrespective of whether or not the authority phases its tendering, large authorities may have to use several to ensure that they are not acting anti-competitively (since the volume of work involved if they used only one contract might be beyond the capacity of many companies in the field).

101. Management of many dual use centres will be exempt from CCT. Some authorities may, however, wish to voluntarily expose management of such facilities to competition. In other cases dual use facilities may not be exempt, either because the necessary local education authority powers have not been used to provide them or because they have not been used exclusively by educational establishments for the required minimum number of hours. These issues are discussed further in Chapter 4. A clear understanding of how dual centres are to be treated is, however, essential before contract strategy decisions are made.

102. The major choice when letting more than one contract is between a functional approach, i.e. different contracts for indoor sports centres, outdoor sports, tennis courts, golf courses, etc. and a geographical one in which one contract covers all facilities in a particular area. The best approach will depend upon the mix of facilities an authority provides; golf courses, major tennis centres, ice rinks and other specialist facilities may require different expertise than indoor sports halls and pools and dictate the use of functional contracts, possibly on an area or site basis if the authority has several specialist facilities. An area approach might be best where an authority

has several indoor centres. Westminster City Council has five indoor sites and uses one company to manage two, and another company three. It is able to compare performance and has the option of using one contractor for all five centres if the other operator should fail.

THE CONTRACT SPECIFICATION

103. The specification translates policy and strategy decisions into contract requirements. It should clearly define the overall service objectives so that any contractor knows what is expected and describe, in detail, the service the authority is seeking to provide and how contractor performance will be assessed. It should also set out the action to be taken if the contractor fails to deliver.

MARKETING

104. Authorities will retain their statutory powers over pricing and programming. The order extending CCT to sports management states that the marketing and promotion of facilities is to be carried out by contractors. But marketing professionals regard decisions on prices and programmes as part of marketing (Exhibit 13). Splitting responsibilities between client and contractor will not be easy but good arrangements are essential if use of contractors is to be successful.

Exhibit 13
MARKETING
Under CCT both the client and the contractor will be involved in marketing decisions

Marketing function	
Product	What services to offer. Depends upon the client's social objectives and upon programming and other requirements in the specification. Decisions can be devolved to the contractor within the client's policy requirements.
Price	What to charge customers. Depends upon the client's social and financial objectives and thus upon requirements set out in the specification. Pricing decisions cannot be devolved to contractors.
Place	Where to offer the service. Largely determined by where the facility has been provided. Use of the facility may however need to be promoted in particular parts of the authority to encourage take up by groups the council is particularly trying to help.
Promotion	Persuading people to use what's on offer. Under CCT the contractor is responsible for promoting use of the facility.

105. Decisions should recognise that, as CCT contracts will run for four to six years, no detailed programme and set of prices drawn up in advance is likely to be valid at the end of the contract. Arrangements which lead to better marketing, and increased use, without harming target groups are likely to help meet social objectives. Some of the options are described below.

106. *Programming.* Good marketing involves offering new services as customers' requirements change. Sports centre management may be well placed to do this but may not find it easy if it takes months to agree the smallest change in use. Since increased use, within policy

guidelines, is likely to promote social objectives, detailed client control of programming might be counter productive.

107. Programming decisions might therefore be devolved to contractors. Some authorities are concerned about doing this, fearing that the operator might close a facility at times when it had few users, programme only the most popular activities, make no provision for excellence, or favour club bookings where these provide a guaranteed income and reduce staffing.

108. In almost all existing contracts the authority specifies opening times to guard against closure when use is low. Some give minimum times to allow the addition of, for example, early morning sessions for commuters if the demand exists. Authorities can also specify when a centre must be shut, to guard against late night nuisances to local residents.

Exhibit 14
PROGRAMMING OPTIONS
A range of options is used in existing contracts

Tight control by the client		Little control by the client
Client specifies the programme to be used at the start of the contract. All subsequent changes have to be agreed beforehand by members.	Client provides a policy framework – percentages of time to devote to particular activities; maximum amounts of time to be given over to club use; 'core times' to be kept for casual public use etc. Programme changes which comply with these constraints do not need to be referred to the client for approval.	The client simply specifies that the contractor provide 'a balanced programme'. The contractor makes all programming decisions, meeting regularly with the client to check whether the client views the programme as balanced.
Contractor has no discretion		Contractor has great discretion

109. Otherwise, existing contracts cover the range from detailed client side control to devolution of most responsibility to the operator (Exhibit 14) and include arrangements in which:

— the specification sets out the programme to be used when the contract begins. All subsequent variations are agreed in advance by members;

— the programme is set in advance but a client side officer, rather than members, agrees variations to avoid delays caused by committee cycles;

— the authority provides a framework within which the contractor has discretion – for example, a specified minimum percentage of use must be casual public use; there must always be casual public use at defined 'core' times; some defined minimum percentage of 'core' time must be public use and so on. Minimum times for particular activities can also be specified and bookings and time slots available to the authority's sports development or outreach teams, for schools and so on allowed for in the contract. Authorities can also specify the maximum number of times a year a facility can be put to non-sporting use e.g. a hall used for antique fairs, sales promotions and so on;

— the client offers only broad guidance, for example that there must be a balanced programme with a wide range of activities for all sections of the community. The contractor makes the detailed choices. This requires mutual trust and a clear understanding of each other's philosophy.

Other approaches are also possible. The client might, for example, agree a schedule of rates for certain activities or services which are not required at contract start but may be required later (e.g. the availability of a pool in the early morning for use by potential champions).

110. Though each authority will make its own choice, the two ends of the range contain dangers – restrictions on marketing and exploitation by contractors. Intermediate approaches will often be best.

111. *Prices.* A similar range of options ranging from full client control to substantial devolution might appear possible. However, authorities do not currently possess the power to devolve pricing decisions to contractors.

112. Authorities need, however, to ensure that their control over prices does not hinder the marketing of facilities. Contractors' ability rapidly to devise and introduce new activities, in response to changing public needs, will be reduced if the client's agreement to proposed prices involves lengthy bureaucratic procedures.

113. Current contracts usually give the operator the freedom to charge lower prices than those set by the client and thus to offer off-peak and other discounts.

114. In such circumstances programming requirements such as the opening hours specified by the authority can help to manage pricing. If a pool must be open during the day, the contractor has to heat it, light it, purify the water, open the changing facilities, and provide lifeguards and receptionists. Outside school holidays, the people free to go swimming during a weekday are the unemployed, the retired, parents at home with young children and so on. The contractor may have to charge off-peak prices such people can afford, because otherwise there will be no income to set against these costs.

FINANCIAL ARRANGEMENTS

115. Under CCT the client will deal directly with debt charges and external building maintenance, while the contractor will meet other costs – employees, internal maintenance, energy, water charges, rates etc. Similar arrangements are used in many existing contracts. Six main approaches are used to provide the contractor with income to help meet these costs and generate a profit – franchise arrangements, deficit guarantees possibly with profit or income sharing, risk sharing and open book management fees (Exhibit 15 overleaf).

Exhibit 15
FINANCIAL OPTIONS
There is a range of options

OPTION	CLIENT	CONTRACTOR
Franchise	Meets debt charges and external maintenance of buildings.	Meets other costs. Retains income from users. Pays a fee to the client.
Deficit guarantee	Meets debt charges and the external maintenance of buildings. Pays fee to the contractor.	Meets other costs. Retains income from users and uses this and the fee to meet costs and provide profit.
Profit sharing deficit guarantee	Meets debt charges and external maintenance of buildings. Pays fee to the contractor.	Meets other costs. Retains income from users and uses this and the fee to meet costs and provide profit. Pays a proportion of any profit to the client.
Income sharing deficit guarantee	Meets debt charges and external maintenance of buildings. Pays fee to the contractor.	Meets other costs. Retains income from users and uses this and the fee to meet costs and provide profit. Pays a proportion of income to the client irrespective of whether or not the operation is profitable.
Risk sharing	Meets debt charges and external maintenance of buildings. Meets a proportion of any operating loss.	Meets other costs. Retains income from users. Shares any profit with the client.
Open book management fee	Meets debt charges and external maintenance of buildings. Meets contractor's costs. Pays contractor a fee.	Passes all income to the client.

116. Franchising (Exhibit 16 on p.38) can be used when income from users is expected to exceed the operator's costs. The contractor retains all income and pays the authority for the privilege of running the facility, making a profit if running costs and the authority's fee are less than income, and a loss if outgoings exceed income. The council's fee can be a flat (possibly inflation linked) sum, a percentage of income, a percentage of operator's profit or a mixture. The authority has either a guaranteed income, or one which rises as performance improves, to set against debt charges and other client costs. The approach may be used for golf courses and other operations expected to generate a surplus. Havering uses this approach at its Romford Ice Rink – the operator pays the Council a fixed sum each year; the authority also takes all the operating profit up to an agreed limit; profits above that level are shared on an agreed percentage basis.

117. Many local authority facilities will continue to need a subsidy. Approaches used in existing contracts include:

— so called 'deficit guarantee' arrangements whereby the authority pays a fixed, usually inflation- linked sum (the deficit guarantee) into the contractor's operating account. The operator uses this, together with income from users and sales income, to meet operating expenses, retaining any surplus as profit and meeting any losses (Exhibit 17 overleaf). The tender for the contract is then the 'deficit guarantee' required, which is similar to the subsidy the authority currently gives the facility but with one essential difference — the authority knows in advance exactly what the subsidy will be. The contractor has a strong incentive to increase use as it retains the income. Providing this is done within the authority's policy guidelines, this should also help meet social objectives. The authority cannot however reduce its financial commitment as the contractor takes all the profit if performance is better than expected;

— a variation on this approach provides for some of the profit to be returned to the authority but with the contractor again bearing all losses if performance is poorer than expected (Exhibit 18 on p.39). This reduces the overall cost to the authority when performance is good and is some safeguard against windfall profits to the operator. It also, however, reduces the operator's incentive to increase use. An income sharing variation is possible (Exhibit 19 on p.39); the authority receives back an agreed percentage of gross income (again possibly on a sliding scale) with the rest plus the 'deficit guarantee' being used to meet the contractor's costs and provide profits. The contractor again bears the loss if performance is poorer than anticipated;

— risk sharing (Exhibit 20 on p.40) has been used when both parties — client and contractor — have made substantial capital investments in the site. The authority shares income or operating profit with the operator but also shares operating account losses. It may meet a proportion of the losses if the operating account is in deficit; its commitment is then open ended but, as it underwrites only some losses, the operator still has a powerful incentive to avoid a deficit. Alternatively the contractor can meet the first losses up to some agreed level and the authority the rest;

— a similar approach to the 'open book' management contracts favoured by some catering operators (Exhibit 21 on p.40). The authority pays the contractor a fee, which it retains irrespective of whether or not the operating account is in profit. The authority retains all profit and meets all losses on that account. The contractor has no incentive to increase use and the authority bears all the risk. Some contractors understandably favour such arrangements for facilities expected to show an operating loss. They may appear more attractive to authorities if the facility is likely to show an operating profit. In reality they contain dangers as the contractor has no incentive to make an operating profit and the authority will bear the loss.

118. Combinations of these are also possible; for example the operating account used in risk sharing contracts can include a deficit guarantee paid by the authority.

119. The choice of financial arrangement cannot be made in isolation. Contractors asked to accept risk when the client has retained tight control over programming, one of the main influences over profitability, may ask for high 'deficit guarantees'. Contractors may also ask for increases in guarantees when clients seek changes in programme or prices during contract life. This emphasises the need for flexibility in the specification.

Exhibit 16

FRANCHISING

The contractor pays the authority for the privilege of running the facility, retains income from users and uses this to meet expenses and provide a profit

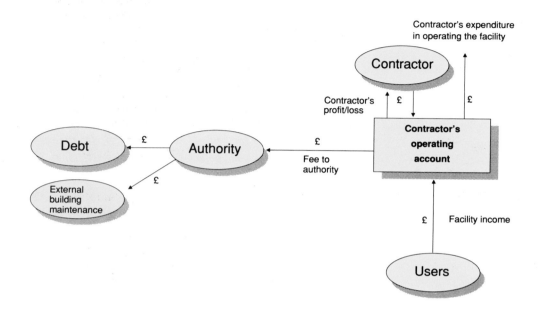

Exhibit 17

FIXED SUBSIDY OR 'DEFICIT GUARANTEE' CONTRACTS

The contractor uses the fee from the authority and the income from users to meet operating expenses and provide profits

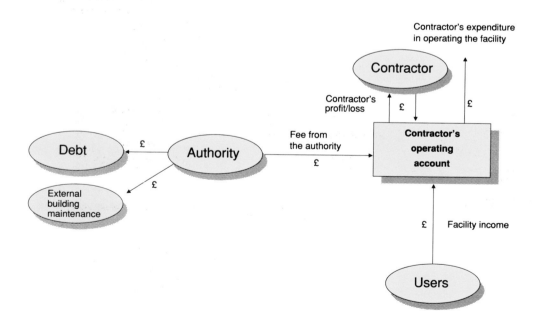

Exhibit 18
PROFIT SHARING 'DEFICIT GUARANTEE' CONTRACTS
The contractor uses the 'deficit guarantee' and income from the users to meet expenses and provide the operating profit; a share of any profit is returned to the authority

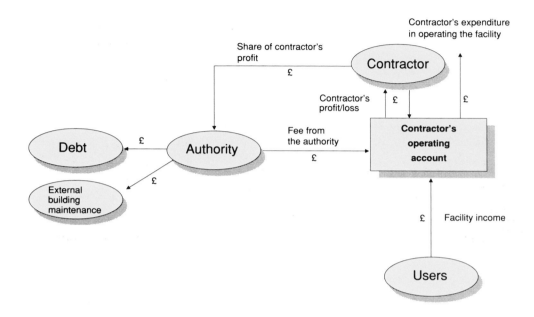

Exhibit 19
INCOME SHARING 'DEFICIT GUARANTEE' CONTRACTS
The contractor uses the 'deficit guarantee' and income from users to meet expenses and provide profits. A share of income is returned to the authority

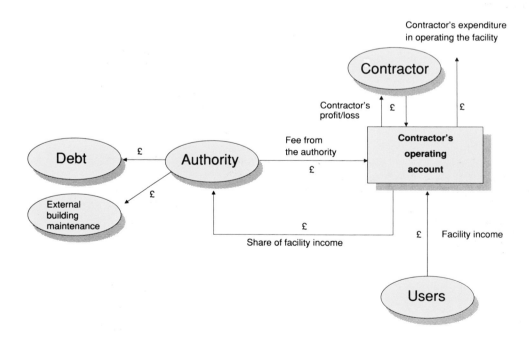

Exhibit 20

RISK SHARING CONTRACTS

Profits or losses on the operating account are shared by the authority and contractor

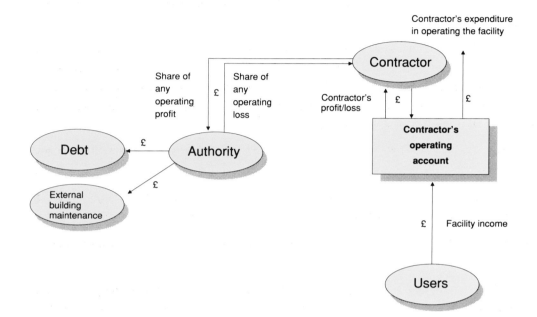

Exhibit 21

OPEN BOOK MANAGEMENT FEE CONTRACTS

The contractor has no incentive to increase use and facility income nor any incentive to control operating costs

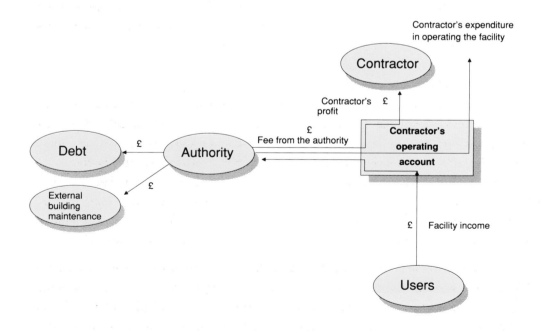

120.   Authorities should not normally use contracts under which the council bears losses if the operator's performance is poorer than expected. They not only make poor financial sense but defeat one purpose of the legislation, the introduction of a businesslike approach to managing sports facilities. Open book management fee arrangements and shared risk contracts should therefore be avoided.

121.   The contractor's performance has financial implications for the authority under all of these arrangements except for the fixed deficit guarantee approach. Contractors' accounts must therefore be inspected and verified. This has, however, proved difficult and costly in internal auditors' time in some existing arrangements where, with hindsight, treatment of costs and income could have been better defined. Examples include:

— interest on income from season ticket sales could either be credited to the operating account or retained by the contractor;

— it was unclear in one case whether group purchase discounts on bar and catering goods should be credited to the operating account;

— directors' remuneration might minimise the operating profit and give a higher share of income to the owners;

— inter-group trading, including use of sister companies to maintain equipment, and franchising (e.g. letting a health suite within a centre to a sister company) and preferential lettings to the operators' friends, family and associates might have a similar effect. The operator's central recharges might also be used to depress operating profitability.

122.   Contract management of leisure facilities is relatively new and some trial and error is to be expected. These difficulties do, however, emphasise just how undesirable it is for the authority to underwrite unexpected operating account losses. They also reveal how easy it might be to depress operating profitability in profit sharing contracts. Income sharing arrangements are easier to check (as the authority only has to audit the income) and at least one authority has switched to income sharing from profit sharing for this reason.

PLANT AND INTERNAL MAINTENANCE

123.   Under CCT the responsibilities for building maintenance will be shared between the authority (external maintenance) and the contractor (other maintenance). A similar arrangement is used in some existing contracts where it is also usual for the authority to be responsible for replacing major plant (heating, air conditioning, boilers etc.) but for the contractor to be responsible for its day to day maintenance. A number of such contracts have been amended as both sides have become aware of the need for clear definitions of current condition, future maintenance regimes, and expected life, to prevent argument in the event of unexpected failures and to avoid dispute about whether plant is in an acceptable condition at contract end.

124.   Contracts should list clearly the plant to be maintained by the operator, set out the maintenance regime and the maintenance records to be kept by the operator together with the client's right of inspection of both plant itself and of the records. A schedule of dilapidation describing condition and expected life is needed. A third party assessor may be used to draw this up.

41

125. The contract should also identify planned major repairs or plant replacement which the client will fund, when work is to be carried out and how long it will take, how the contractor will be recompensed if work takes longer than expected and any clawback the authority is to receive if the work takes less time than anticipated.

126. Authorities similarly need to make clear the condition they expect to find the interior of the building in when the contract expires. Requirements can be broadly similar to those in landlord and tenant agreements. Westminster City Council's contracts, for example, include a detailed redecoration programme.

127. Responsibilities for minor plant and equipment (e.g. gymnastic equipment) also need to be set out. These might be provided initially by the authority but replaced by the contractor. An inventory describing condition is again needed together with replacement guidelines.

CAPITAL INVESTMENT

128. Although local authority sports facilities do not usually provide an economic return on capital there are circumstances in which contractors may be willing to invest in equipment. The Crossland group has, for example, installed fitness studio, sun-bed, sauna and spa bath equipment in sports centres under its management.

129. Tender documents can therefore request investment proposals from prospective contractors (though requiring investment might lead to allegations of anti- competitiveness). This will, however, complicate tender evaluation as different operators may make radically different proposals. Another difficulty is that the authority may not wish to see equipment removed when the contract ends. One solution is to agree a depreciation formula and give the client the right to purchase the equipment at residual value.

130. Authorities entering such arrangements should ensure that this does not hinder their ability to manage the operator. Early termination is the ultimate sanction for failure to perform but is meaningless if the contractor knows that the authority is unable to buy the remaining life of a large investment. Authorities need similarly to ensure that they do not restrict their ability to retender competitively at contract end.

131. DSOs might be at a disadvantage when capital investment is requested as any investment they made would be a capital investment by the local authority and subject to controls on capital expenditure. Any investment they could offer might as well be made by the authority before contracts are let. Authorities can, however, enter leasing arrangements on behalf of DSOs which successor operators could take over at the end of the contract.

CONTRACT PERIOD

132. Authorities operating outside CCT have more freedom of action and can offer longer contracts than the four to six years required under the regulations. Though there are circumstances where longer periods may be appropriate, for example to attract major private

investment in a facility, the CCT range should be used where possible. Sport and leisure fashions are volatile and any detailed arrangements are unlikely to be valid for ten or twenty years. Authorities using long contracts may find it difficult to resist changes favourable to contractors and will lose out on the further improvements in price and performance which retendering after 4 - 6 years is likely to offer.

PERFORMANCE BONDS

133. Performance bonds and holding company guarantees offer safeguards against contractor failure. Authorities should draw up contingency plans to cover failure and use these to identify the likely extra costs (i.e. the costs above those normally incurred by the service). These costs can form the basis of a performance bond or guarantee.

134. Some contractors might be deterred by the need to give a bond, and it is likely that contract prices may be higher than otherwise to cover the cost of raising it. Very large bonds (in relation to contract value) could therefore be anti-competitive, as indicated in DOE circular 19/88 and Welsh Office circular 39/88.

OTHER CONTRACTUAL ISSUES

135. Other important issues include:

— energy. Differences between predicted and actual energy consumption in some new buildings have also required renegotiation, for example in the quasi- contractual arrangement at Chichester. Again, fees might be renegotiated, though a third party survey might first be needed to ensure that higher costs are not being caused by poor energy management by the contractor. Authorities should re-appraise energy use and introduce any energy saving measures before contracts are let otherwise contractors who spot opportunities for savings will make windfall profits while, on other occasions, contractors may be able to prevent the introduction by the authority of measures which have a longer payback period than remaining contract life;

— advertising. Surrey Heath (Arena Centre) and Havering (Romford Ice Rink) require that advertisements be agreed with the authority. Both contracts were let voluntarily, outside CCT. Care is needed to ensure that client side control does not constrain the operator's marketing and promotion of the facility;

— any restrictions on fruit machines, video games, etc. Some authorities will want explicitly to forbid installation or limit either the numbers of machines or where they are placed e.g. restricting them to bar areas;

— compliance with health and safety and public health legislation. Some current contracts, for example, specify minimum qualification standards for pool attendants. Others set out air and pool temperatures, water conditions etc. in detail. Many authorities will be particularly concerned about lifeguarding arrangements in pools. It is open to authorities to specify such arrangements in detail but the specification must not extend to specifying terms and conditions of employment of the lifeguards. Failure to ensure adequate lifeguarding arrangements may, of course, give rise to both criminal and civil liability on the part of both the authority and the contractor. Authorities would be well advised to obtain an indemnity covering civil liability from the contractor in the contract documentation. The possibility of such liabilities emphasises the need properly to specify and supervise lifeguarding and other safety arrangements;

— responsibilities for insurance, covering structural repair, any loss to the contractor as a result of structural failure etc.;

— availability of halls during emergencies and elections. Some existing contracts give the authority first call for these purposes without recompense to the contractor;

— default point and liquidated damages conditions.

INFORMATION TO INCLUDE IN THE SPECIFICATION

136. Contractors can prepare tenders only if they have a good understanding of likely operating costs and income. Tenderers should be told the current and past programmes of use and pricing regimes and be given details of either income or total usage under each of the main activities over the last three to five years. The client should also make available data on catchment areas and population gathered during the strategy review. The DSO is likely to have the advantage of having seen it. Tenderers should also be allowed to inspect plant and maintenance records, to help assess maintenance costs and confirm the schedule of dilapidation. They should also be aware of current rate, energy, water and other service costs and be able to inspect relevant parts of the facility (since savings they believe they might make by, for example, better energy management are relevant to their bid).

137. Opening hours and safety requirements, any coaching needs and other requirements likely to affect staffing should be clearly specified and prospective tenderers given supervised access to facilities to help in their assessment of staffing needs.

138. One approach to information is to require the successful tenderer to provide the client, throughout the contract, with similar data to that made available with the specification, making clear that the client expects to make this available to other bidders when the contract comes up for renewal.

DISCUSSIONS WITH CONTRACTORS

139. Authorities should approach contractors before finalising their approach to ascertain the type of contracts (functional or area, including or excluding catering etc.) likely to generate most interest and the amount of work with which they are able to cope. The newly formed Leisure Contractors' Association may be able to help. An alternative is to offer a separate contract for each major site and to allow tenderers to bid for one or more as they see fit. Each will be able to select the locations which it finds most attractive. Bids should then reflect any economies of scale, while the authority will be able to select the offers which give it the lowest overall price.

SHORT LIST AND TENDER EVALUATION

140. The authority must invite tenders from at least three private contractors where more than three wish to bid. It must invite bids from all those interested if three or fewer wish to tender. Under the Local Government Act 1988, if DSOs from other authorities are invited to bid, this must be in addition to, rather than instead of, the specified number of private contractors.

141.   The compilation of a short list may well present problems. The number of sports management contracts will increase by several thousand percent between 1989 and 1993. The ten or so existing UK contractors cannot realistically be expected to take on all this work. Contractors from other countries in the European Community may try to enter the UK market. This is already happening for other services covered by CCT, such as refuse collection and street cleansing; contractors manage sports facilities in, for example, the Netherlands and representatives of Dutch companies have visited the UK to examine the sports management market . Newly formed companies which lack a financial history and proven expertise may also bid; established, financially sound organisations may also try to enter this new market, but will lack a relevant track record.

142.   Sometimes a local authority will not be able to avoid inviting a patently unfit contractor to tender.   In such cases the CIPFA *Code of practice for compulsory competition* recommends that the authority should advise the contractor when inviting it to tender that there are certain factors unrelated to the tender which in the authority's opinion render it unsuitable. The contractor then does not need to waste time preparing a tender. Authorities will need sound reasons for taking this course of action to avoid charges of anti-competitiveness.

143.   Authorities should document formal evaluation methods in advance of short listing and tender evaluation. Some have, for example, developed tender vetting questionnaires for other services to help choose the competent contractors and check that the winning tender is in order. At the first stage these ask for general information on company status, accounts and previous work, and for specific information on items such as health and safety arrangements. At the second stage they require specific details on matters such as supervisory arrangements and arrangements to cover for unexpected sickness or leave among staff. The methodologies can be adapted for sports management.

144.   Authorities should meet potential contractors between sending out specifications and the contractor completing the tender, to make sure that the contractor fully understands what is required. The authority may also visit contractors' current sites.

145.   At tender evaluation, authorities should ask contractors for specific details of how a contract would be operated and managed*. The procedure should require presentations from tenderers, describing how they expect to operate facilities, followed by question and answer sessions. Contractors should be asked to submit outline marketing plans. The importance of the expertise offered means that authorities should formally interview senior staff, and their expertise and suitability be assessed using criteria similar to those previously employed when making an in-house appointment. The authority should also consider how vulnerable a tenderer is to the loss of one or two key personnel.

146.   Evaluation will present another problem. Under most contracts tenderers' prices will be based not simply on an estimate of operating cost but also on an estimate of the income to be generated, which in turn depends on the tenderers' predictions of the number of users they expect to attract to the facility. An over-optimistic assessment may mean that an operator will not receive the income needed to cover costs and may fail or withdraw part of the way during contract

---

*   *The Accounting Code of Practice in CIPFA's 'Meeting the challenge' sets out the issues which can and cannot be taken into account in CIPFA's view when choosing contractors to tender.*

life. Leisure usage predictions are, however, notoriously unreliable and estimates from well established, reputable operators bidding for the same contract can differ markedly.

147. Authorities can estimate realistic ranges for operating costs, usage and income before opening tenders. Quotes falling outside the ranges should be thoroughly investigated for realism. The ranges should take account of the performances achieved by the best authorities; competition has improved performance and reduced costs in other services and is likely to have the same effect in sports management. Authorities might also decide, before opening tenders, to seek further details from any bidder whose price differs from that of the second lowest tenderer by more than a pre-determined amount.

148. Authorities should not, however, reject an unexpectedly low price, or high franchise offer, without thoroughly investigating the viability of that quote. Professional expertise is therefore needed on the client side to help with tender evaluation. This will be a problem for smaller authorities which have adopted the 'two hatted' approach to client-contractor roles; the chief officer may have been too involved in preparing the DSO bid to help with evaluation. These and other authorities may need to buy in consultancy advice to help with evaluation.

149. Profit sharing contracts further complicate the process. Authorities must decide whether to make their financial assessment on the maximum cost to the client (e.g. on the worst case assumption that the operating account shows a loss and that the authority therefore receives no profit share to set against the 'deficit guarantee' it has paid the contractor) or on most likely cost (e.g. the 'deficit guarantee' less expected profit share). Assessments of income sharing bids face similar problems; the client's assessment of the contractor's predicted use is central to the evaluation. Allegations of anti-competitive behaviour may be made if a DSO wins a profit or income sharing contract against private sector operators which have predicted a higher income for the authority than the DSO has. This emphasises the need fully to explore tenderers' marketing proposals and usage predictions.

150. Evaluations should be fully documented. One option when examining qualitative issues is PAG (Poor, Average, Good) analysis. Each bid is marked independently by each member of the evaluation panel under a series of subjective headings receiving one mark if poor, three if average, five if good. Points are totalled to help with evaluation. This methodology (including the headings to use and the minimum score needed to be adjudged a viable contractor) should also be formally agreed before tenders are evaluated. The approach to short list and tender evaluation is summarised in Exhibit 22.

151. If an outside contractor submits the lowest bid the authority is faced with the question of redundancy payments to its own workforce. The Commission has issued advice to its auditors on how redundancy and certain other costs may be taken into consideration.

CONTRACT START UP

152. The authority should have plans for the handover of facilities, equipment and possibly employees to a successful outside contractor, and for handling redundancies. The starting date should, if possible, not be at a particularly busy or inconvenient time such as a bank holiday in spring or early summer. Start up arrangements should be set out in the specification. If the DSO or existing contractor has lost there is a danger that staff morale will fall and standards decline

Exhibit 22
CONTRACTOR VETTING AND TENDER EVALUATION
These procedures will help ensure that authorities award contracts to competent and efficient contractors

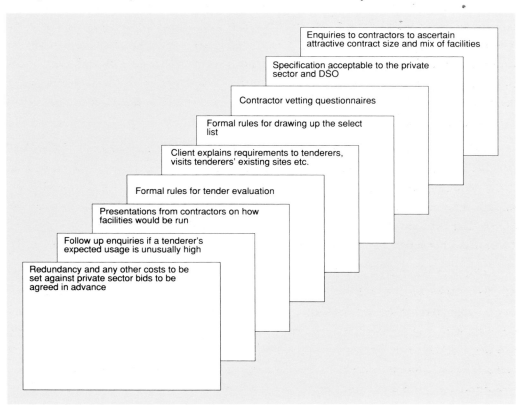

Enquiries to contractors to ascertain attractive contract size and mix of facilities

Specification acceptable to the private sector and DSO

Contractor vetting questionnaires

Formal rules for drawing up the select list

Client explains requirements to tenderers, visits tenderers' existing sites etc.

Formal rules for tender evaluation

Presentations from contractors on how facilities would be run

Follow up enquiries if a tenderer's expected usage is unusually high

Redundancy and any other costs to be set against private sector bids to be agreed in advance

between the announcement and the start of the new contract. Authorities need to take account of this, and the dangers to staff morale of uncertainty, when preparing their timetables for implementing CCT.

153.   Some teething troubles are inevitable when a service is reorganised. The client should recognise this and promote as smooth a transition as possible. There should be a phasing-in period for the default system. Only in extreme instances should there be any threat of early contract termination. The purpose should instead be to ensure that after a period of, say, one month the service is operating reasonably and in line with specification. The full default system can then be applied.

SUPERVISION AND MANAGEMENT

154.   The management of many existing contracts is weak. Some authorities receive no usage information; two visited during the study suggested that the Commission's project team contact their management company directly to obtain the information. Such authorities have little, if any, idea of what they are achieving for the money they spend or how the contractor's performance compares with the national picture.

155.   Information is not needed solely to check whether the authority's aims are being met. It is also needed to verify payments in profit, income or loss sharing arrangements. In addition retendering, either at contract end, or earlier if the contractor has failed, is central to the client's

control of the service. The client must therefore be able to provide the information needed by prospective tenderers.

156. Since the verification of contractors' accounts in profit, income or loss sharing contracts can be difficult and costly, authorities using these approaches should consider specifying the form of the accounts and, in profit or loss sharing arrangements, how overheads, discounts, interest on income, directors' payments, intergroup trading, franchising and lettings to operators' friends, family and associates and so on should be treated. The maximum number of directors and maximum directors' remuneration that the authority is prepared to take into account in calculating profit can also be specified. Authorities which have installed computerised tills, management information and accounting systems might require their continued use by the successful tenderer and might even retain read-only access.

157. Compliance with plant maintenance, health and safety legislation, public health, opening hours, programming, pricing and water condition and temperature requirements also needs to be examined. Records to be maintained (e.g. user injuries, details of staff training and qualifications) can be specified together with the client's right of access to facilities and records. The right of internal and external auditors to check usage information and, in profit or income sharing arrangements, to check operating account details at source should also be mentioned; tenderers new to local government may not be aware of auditors' statutory powers.

158. Poor contractor performance will defeat authorities' social aims. Effectiveness reviews should therefore be allowed for in contracts. Value for money reviews should also be allowed in profit, income and loss sharing arrangements; even though accounts may be correct, poor contractor performance will deprive the authority of money. Where DSOs win work their performance needs similarly to be reviewed; poor performance again defeats social objectives. The authority should also encourage its DSO to maximise its profit, while adhering to the contract, because this profit can be used by the authority.

159. User satisfaction can also be monitored (via, for example, occasional client side surveys). The contractor might even receive a small bonus if satisfaction levels were above a specified minimum. The two sides should regularly meet to discuss problems, particularly if the contractor has discretion in programming. In the longer term quality assurance under British Standard 5750 is another option and one which may reduce client side supervision costs. Though certification for sports management is not yet possible, the position may change by the early 1990s; a leisure sub-committee has been established by the British Quality Association's Local Government Sector Quality Committee to review the application of the standard to local authorities' leisure services.

PERFORMANCE AND POLICY REVIEW

160. Performance monitoring involves checking not only that the contractor is meeting the specification but that the wider objectives of the service are being met. The data and mechanisms needed for this will have been identified in the strategy review. Members should receive regular reports on the level of public satisfaction with sports provision and sports facility operations. This can be done both reactively, by monitoring complaints, and pro-actively, by public opinion surveys. Such information will complement reports on contractor performance

(for example data on attendances) and help provide an overall picture of the service. Client side staffing and budgets should take account of this. Any information the contractor is to provide to help with performance and policy review should be set out in the specification.

✲   ✲   ✲

161. This chapter has discussed the competitive tendering process. The points made are summarised in Exhibit 23. The next chapter discusses the changes DSOs need to make in order to compete realistically.

Exhibit 23
THE CLIENT ROLE UNDER CCT
Under CCT the client has a crucial role to play

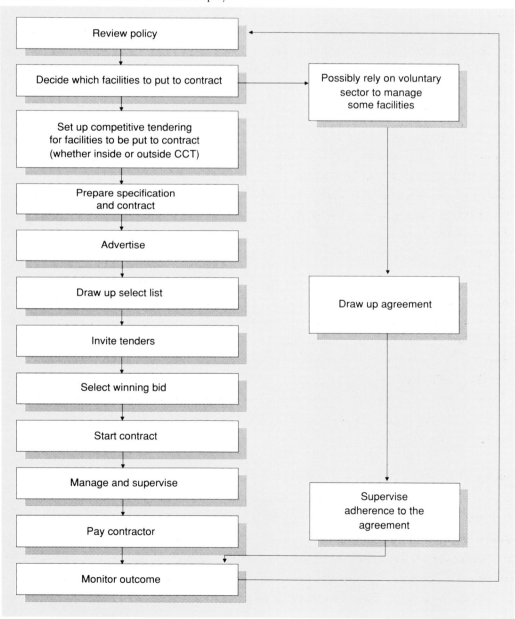

3. Preparing the DSO for Competition

162. Competition alone may not be sufficient to ensure keen prices. The most efficient contractors may not bid, or contractors may pitch their bids at what the local market will bear rather than the lowest price at which they can make a reasonable profit. Evidence from the Commission's studies of building and highways maintenance suggests that authorities tend to obtain better prices, irrespective of who wins, when efficient DSOs bid against the private sector.

163. The Commission therefore regards the existence of efficient DSOs as beneficial. But many recreation DSOs need to improve their performance to be competitive. Experience from other services suggests that they may need to achieve or beat the performance now obtained by the best 10% of in-house operations if they are to stand a chance of success in a truly competitive tender. The limited experience to date of contracting out of sports management supports this assessment. Major changes in attitudes, style and conditions of service will often be needed.

164. The DSO's central objectives are to win work and then to meet its statutory financial target. Some DSOs will not bid for some of the contracts offered by their authority, in the belief that they cannot both offer a winning price and then make their rate of return. Others will be required to bid for contracts they find unattractive – to provide their authority with a contractor of last resort if no one else bids or if all other offers are very expensive – but will put in high tenders, to ensure they meet their financial target if awarded the work. Once work has been won, the DSO needs to identify and exploit every opportunity to increase income within the programming and pricing constraints set by the client.

165. The DSO needs to guard against overstaffing. Pay and conditions of service should reflect the state of the local labour market. Other costs, including overheads, should also be controlled. DSO managers will need delegated authority, including greater control over budgets and expenditure; standing orders may need to be amended. Management information systems should be tailored to their needs.

MARKETING

166. Though marketing of local authority sports facilities is improving, the weaknesses identified by Pannell Kerr Forster in their work for the Audit Inspectorate in 1983 are still common. Marketing is more than advertising; it is the whole process of deciding what service to provide, whom to provide it for, what prices to charge, how to persuade people to use the services and how to monitor success. Promotion is a part of marketing, persuading people to use services; and advertising is one, but only one, way of promoting use.

DECIDING WHAT SERVICES TO OFFER

167. The client's specification will give considerable guidance on services. Most contracts will, however, give the DSO some discretion and some will allow great freedom of action. DSOs

51

should exploit such opportunities and should develop ideas even when prior client approval is required for changes in programming and even though client agreement is needed on prices. A wise client will accept proposals which increase use while remaining consistent with its policy objectives.

168.   The DSO needs to decide whether its objectives are, for example:

— simply to sell use of the facility;

— to add to the sports experience, for example by providing coaching and learners' sessions;

— to provide a wider leisure experience of which sport is only a part. Bar and catering facilities will then be important as will the 'added value' of, for example, parent and child swim sessions followed by coffee and biscuits or children's birthday parties where a group swim is followed by a visit to the cafeteria;

— provide non sporting services, for example, social functions in the bar or cafeteria, wedding receptions, sales promotions, antiques fairs etc. Advertising space in the centre, pavilions etc. can also be sold.

169.   SWOT analysis (strengths, weaknesses, opportunities, threats) can help identify what to provide. Each sports facility will have its own best mix of activities and use depending on its design and catchment population. The DSO should segment the market into different groups and design sessions which appeal to them, within the client's programming constraints. It can only do this if it knows:

— who currently uses facilities, when and what they use them for, whether they are satisfied or not with the service they receive and, if not, why they are dissatisfied;

— who would like to use facilities but does not and why not;

— which people do not use the facility, either because they use alternatives or because they are not interested in sport. A lack of interest does not, however, mean that they will not take part if offered a well designed and presented package.

170.   The DSO also needs demographic and geographical information on its catchment population, details of commuter movement (e.g. in town centres), data on local transport and information about its competitors – whether private sector, voluntary sector, company sports clubs or other local authority facilities – and on what they offer and charge.

171.   The client's strategy review should provide much of this data and should be offered to the DSO and private sector tenderers, to help them put together their bids. DSOs can carry out work of their own before preparing bids, if there has not been a review or if there are important gaps in the data. Marketing is an operation throughout contract life and DSOs should carry out market research to update and expand earlier information, once work has been won.

172.   Prices will require the client's consent. In making proposals DSOs should recognise that different groups may be willing and able to pay different charges. For example:

— commuters and business people may be willing to pay well above the normal price for an early morning swim;

— facilities may sometimes be over-subscribed outside normal working hours e.g. weekday evenings or at lunchtime in city centres. Usage may not fall if prices are raised and may even increase if the DSO simultaneously advertises the lower, off-peak price or draws the attention of 'turn aways' to off-peak opportunities;

— many families will pay several pounds a day for daily coaching/sports activities courses during school holidays. Such courses can be highly profitable. The opportunity exists irrespective of social reasons for providing courses (and clients can of course, purchase places on behalf of disadvantaged groups if they wish);

— many people are willing to pay above the normal price of a swim for added value activities, fun sessions with inflatables and so on;

— many facilities are poorly used during the day from Monday to Friday. The unemployed, the retired and other unwaged groups constitute an available market. They may be able to pay only low prices. Schools are another potential market, though charges will have to appear attractive to establishments managing their own budgets.

173. The DSO should therefore try and propose a price for each target group and activity which maximises its income. Drops in use are of no concern to the DSO if income rises, providing it has met its contract; this is for the client to consider when deciding whether to agree a proposed price, or programming, change.

174. DSOs may need to invest in the facilities. For example, a DSO that decides that bar and catering operations, and social and other non-sporting events, are to be major revenue sources may need to invest in new equipment, furniture and redecoration, either by leasing, by using capital provided by the authority or from its operating profit. One which wants to target the health conscious may similarly need to invest in saunas, whirlpool baths, sunbeds and keep fit equipment. Depending on the target markets chosen, DSOs may also need to set up, or franchise out, beauticians, hairdressing salons and sports shops.

175. The steps involved in deciding what to offer and to whom, and the interaction with the client's requirements are summarised in Exhibit 24 (overleaf).

PROMOTION

176. Promotion has two aspects – persuading people to turn up for the first time and persuading them to come back (repeat business). Advertising is one, but only one, way of generating first visits.

177. Advertising material needs to be clear and well designed. Grubby hand-drawn, xeroxed leaflets and posters are unlikely to be very effective (though over-glossy leaflets run the risk of generating resentment at the 'waste of public money'). Desktop publishing software is available for only a few hundred pounds, and can be run on computers used primarily for word processing or management information purposes. Advertisements and other written material should be in the style most appropriate to the target group they are aimed at – facilities likely to be used by commuters, such as early morning swims, may need to be presented in different ways to those mainly used by other groups. Professional design input should be used for large- scale campaigns; students taking the appropriate courses at local colleges are an alternative for smaller campaigns. In some authorities the ethnic mix may mean that at least some advertising should be in languages other than English.

Exhibit 24
THE MARKETING PLAN
To develop a marketing plan DSOs need to follow this procedure

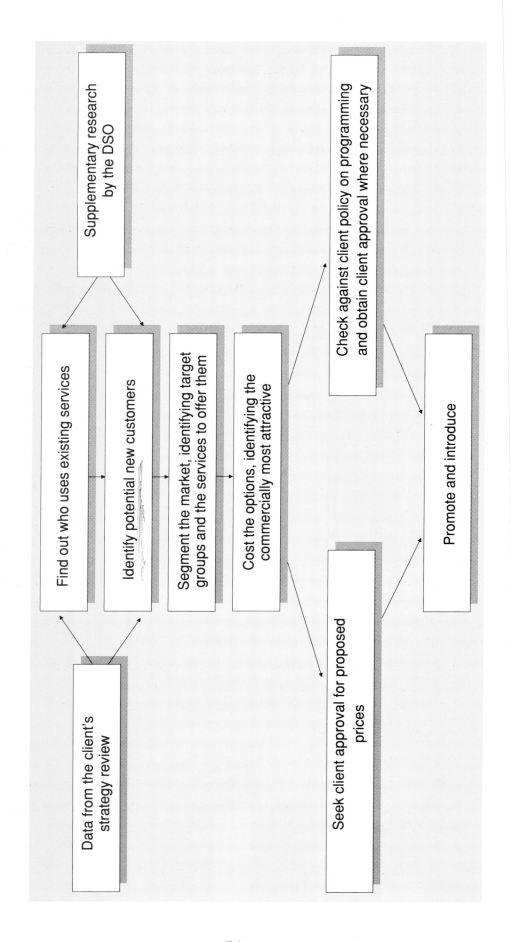

178.   Publicity does not necessarily have to cost money. One authority visited (Chichester District Council) was producing a free local newspaper devoted to sport and recreation at no cost to itself. It provided a local publisher with editorial material; the publisher printed and distributed the paper, meeting costs and making profit from sales of advertising. The authority also obtained considerable local publicity for a new centre by organising a competition to choose the name. Local newspapers, radio and television are sometimes willing to report competitive events, fund raising activities, visits by well known sporting personalities and so on as news events. Successful sportsmen and women and teams can receive excellent local publicity; it may make good commercial sense to support local swimming clubs and champions.

179.   Advertising and press publicity may not be the best way of generating use. The DSO should know which groups it particularly expects to use particular services. It may be best to contact them directly. This can involve approaches to local clubs, leagues and associations; visits to local firms and companies, police and fire stations etc.; visits to schools and youth clubs; contact with women's groups, playschools and creches; direct contact with unemployed groups and with social and other clubs used by the retired; direct approaches to churches and associations used by ethnic groups and so on.

180.   Non-sporting events – antiques fairs, wedding receptions etc. – can play a role. They not only generate income in their own right but can make people aware of a centre for the first time. Special promotions can also be used – free initial swim on production of a leaflet, special low cost introductory coaching sessions to employees of a local firm. Special membership schemes can also be devised that are available only to staff of particular companies, members of particular clubs etc.

181.   But many people make their initial visit to a sports facility because they have heard about it from a friend. This, and the fact that people who have been persuaded to use a facility for the first time and don't enjoy it are unlikely to come back and very likely to tell other prospective customers not to visit the centre, means that quality of service and the way a facility presents itself to customers are central to success. Repeat business is, in other words, essential. Research commissioned by the Sports Council suggests that only a few hundred people a year typically provide the bulk of use of a sports centre*. A single keen sportsman or woman who stops using a centre because they are dissatisfied with it may represent a loss of income from over 100 user visits a year.

182.   Good customer care is thus an essential part of promotion and affects all aspects of the way in which a centre presents itself to the public. For example:

— has the facility a clear image (centre logo, colours, smart staff uniforms etc)?

— are staff polite and helpful?

— do receptionists answer telephone enquiries quickly?

— is the building clean, attractive and well decorated? Is vandal damage quickly repaired?

— are the changing facilities adequate? Do lockers work; are the floors clean and dry; is the shower temperature correct?

---

* Data in 'The Sports Council's standardised approach to sports hall design - SASH centres in use: design and management' prepared for the Sports Council by ECOTEC Research and Consulting Ltd in May 1987.

— are cafeteria clean and in good condition? Is the bar and catering service reliable; do customers know when they will be open? Do operators keep to these times? Do vending machines work and are they filled regularly?

183. Special arrangements may also be needed for particular target groups. Sessions aimed at parents with young children may, for example, require a creche; some companies already managing local authority facilities run these, without being required to do so by their client. People in rural areas may need transport; again some commercially managed centres run their own buses and may, for example, include transport in the package they offer clubs, associations or schools.

RESPONSIBILITY AND BUDGET

184. Marketing cannot be handled in an ad hoc manner. Someone should be designated as marketing manager in all recreation DSOs. It may be a part time function of the DSO manager in the smaller ones but will be full time in larger operations; one person per contract may be needed in the largest authorities. A job description for a marketing manager in a larger DSO appears at Appendix D. However, promotion involves everyone in the DSO, not just the marketing manager. Customer service training sessions may be needed to bring home the new approach.

185. Outside support may have to be brought in to help with the initial reviews of marketing. The marketing manager's responsibilities will, however, be on-going. The manager will have to monitor usage and income on at least a weekly basis, comparing actual and expected use and income on a room by room, session by session basis to spot quickly trends and problems.

186. New services and activities have to be designed and introduced quickly – some opportunities will disappear if initiatives are delayed while approval is sought. The centre or DSO manager, or the client when its approval is needed, should therefore respond quickly to the marketing manager's proposals. The DSO's product has no shelf life; a time slot which is not sold is lost forever.

187. A budget is required for on-going user surveys, advertising and other promotional work. Some authorities still do not provide one; those that do, often underfund, allocating only a few tenths of one percent of gross expenditure. Successful local authority operations, and contractors, devote two or more percent of gross expenditure to marketing.

188. Expenditure on items such as staff uniforms, potted plants, minor repairs and frequent redecoration – perhaps every two to three years – should not be charged to promotion. Supervisors should, however, be prepared to spend on them in line with overall marketing policy.

STAFFING

STAFFING LEVELS

189. Staffing is a major cost, in indoor sports centres in particular (Exhibit 25). The variation in levels (Exhibit 26) suggests that some facilities may be over-staffed. Direct comparisons between public and private sector operations are difficult but Sports Council comparisons between similarly sized private and public sector ice rinks, opened at about the same time, reveal that the more heavily used, and more financially successful, private sector rink had

Exhibit 25
STAFF COSTS
On average, staff costs account for approaching half of gross expenditure (excluding debt costs)

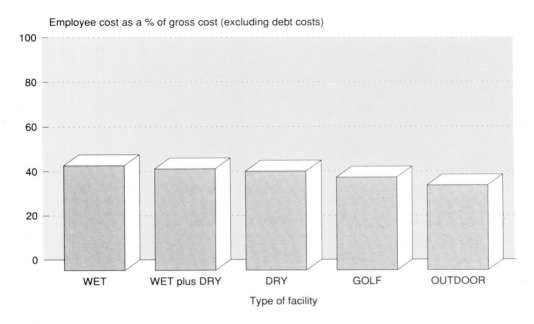

Employee cost as a % of gross cost (excluding debt costs)

Source: Audit Commission analysis of CIPFA 'Leisure and recreation estimates 1988-89'

Exhibit 26
STAFFING VARIATIONS AT SWIMMING POOLS
The number of FTE staff per square metre of water varies markedly from authority to authority

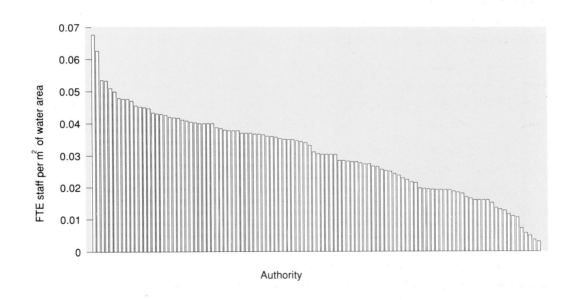

Source: Audit Commission analysis of CIPFA 'Leisure and recreation estimates 1988-89', for authorities with swimming pools but no 'wet plus dry' centres

one third fewer staff than the public sector one. Major staff reductions have certainly been a feature when other services have been put out to tender, irrespective of who wins; staffing reductions of 30% or more are common in refuse collection, for example.

190. Recreation DSOs must ensure that they are not overstaffed. They should set full time levels based on demand at troughs if part timers can be used more economically at peak times. Reviews of staffing will have to take account of, for example, the advice in the Health and Safety Commission/Sports Council publication *Safety in swimming pools*. This recognises that there are circumstances where constant poolside supervision is less likely to be essential, including some types of club use. Club use for other, less potentially dangerous activities may also require fewer staff; careful programming of club sessions so that, for example, they are grouped at the end of the day may reduce staffing needs. Programmes might even be arranged, if the client allows, so that there are club-only sessions when casual public use is lowest.

191. Employees should be used flexibly. A smaller workforce working flexible rosters, supplemented by seasonal and part-time workers can also reduce employers' national insurance and other on-costs. Specialist coaching, required for only a few hours a week may be particularly suitable for part-timers. Holiday arrangements need to be reconsidered, particularly at facilities with a strong seasonal pattern of use; allowing staff to take all, or most, of their annual leave at such times will increase costs.

PAY AND CONDITIONS OF SERVICE

192. Local authorities pride themselves on being good employers. They should, however, avoid being so generous that they damage employees' long term prospects. The overall package – pay, allowances, holidays, sick pay arrangements, superannuation etc. – must reflect the local labour market. This does not necessarily mean a fall in pay. Some contractors claim that their employees are paid more than local authority staff with broadly similar jobs. Bonuses based on financial performance and shared out on the basis of staff appraisal results are an important part of their pay structures. Incentives based on hitting minimum financial targets can similarly be offered to local authority employees and centre managers.

193. Contractors' staff often also receive only basic pay for working rostered shifts; there are no premiums for unsocial hours, irregular hours or nightwork. It is much easier for them to alter the programme offered, arrange sick cover and so on without incurring extra costs. Managers do not have to devote large amounts of time to juggling different staff rostering options to find the one costing the least and can use their time more constructively e.g. to come up with new marketing ideas. Other parts of contractors' employment packages – e.g. leave entitlements – may also be less generous than those now used in local government. DSOs may need to act similarly and to move to local agreements about pay and conditions of service. The issues to be considered when reviewing the employment package are summarised in Exhibit 27.

Exhibit 27
REVIEWING DSO STAFFING COSTS
DSO staffing costs can be reviewed using this approach

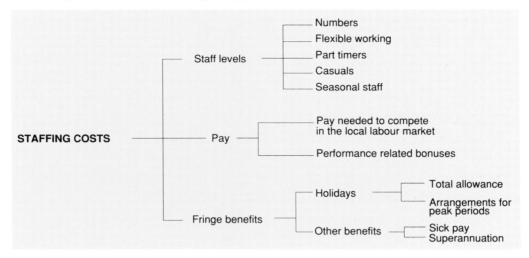

OTHER COSTS
OVERHEADS

194. Financing charges will usually appear either in the client account or in a central committee account, not in the DSO's. In addition CIPFA has said (in *Meeting the challenge*) that there is a good case for exempting DSOs from some of the costs of democracy and has identified elements that it would be illogical to apportion to DSOs.

195. Other items such as finance, management services and legal support costs will be charged to DSOs but can be minimised and controlled by:

— transferring administrative responsibilities to centre management wherever appropriate, and giving management the freedom to decide the staffing levels needed;

— setting up a quasi-trading account relationship between central departments and the DSO in which the DSO acts as client and central departments as contractors. The DSO is then charged an agreed sum per employee for payroll processing, for example, and obtains legal and other specialist advice at an agreed hourly rate. Such service level agreements are discussed in more detail in CIPFA's *Accounting for support services* and *Accounting for support services - a practitioner's guide*. Authorities also have the option of allowing DSOs to buy support services from outside if this is cheaper.

SERVICE AND MINOR MAINTENANCE COSTS

196. The DSO will be responsible for meeting service charges – gas, electricity, water, telephones etc. It will also be responsible for cleaning, catering and ground maintenance, when these activities have been included in management contracts. Its management must be able to control expenditure on these items. It should, for example, be able to initiate energy saving measures where these will prove cost effective. Management should similarly control internal maintenance. Redecoration or rapid repair of vandalism may, for example, be needed to encourage repeat business or simply to allow continued use of the facility. There are still leisure centres where, for example, it takes weeks for the authority's building maintenance DLO to replace missing plaster on a squash court wall; the court cannot, of course, be let until repaired.

DELEGATED RESPONSIBILITY
MANAGEMENT MUST MANAGE

197.   Many local government sports facility managers recognise the need for better marketing, for customer care, for better use of staff and for better cost control but have found these difficult to achieve under existing organisational and financial constraints. Expenditure and income budgets have often been set separately and are often arrived at by simply adjusting last year's figures for inflation. Managers have often had little freedom to vire between heads or to incur extra expenditure if this will generate extra income. They have also had little control over the number of staff they employ and their conditions of service, over the central and departmental recharges they bear or over the maintenance, cleaning and service costs of the buildings they run.

198.   CCT alters the position. Net profit or loss, not the fine detail of the budget, is the overriding financial consideration. The DSO must be given the freedom to manage within the constraints of the authority's objectives and the client's policies. DSO managers can then act in an businesslike way, and respond to market trends, in consultation with their client. Good local authority sports and recreation arrangements already give on-site management teams this delegated authority.

199.   The role of members needs to change, especially where they have had a significant impact on the day to day running of the business; DSO competitiveness will be severely hindered if every operational decision has to be referred to the committee or board or if members attempt to become involved in day to day management. DSO board or committee members should concentrate on setting policy objectives and then on monitoring performance to ensure they are met. Board members should not allow a DSO to rest on its laurels because it has won work and is in profit. They should view the DSO as a business 'owned' by the authority and, as its representatives, seek the best possible return from the DSO. Members' complaints about service levels and quality should be made to the client committee or officer, not the DSO board or DSO manager.

FINANCIAL CONTROL

200.   Allowing management to manage means delegating financial control to the DSO. This does not mean abandoning budget processes, financial monitoring, accountability for expenditure and the need for audit trails. It simply requires the freedom to make properly documented adjustments to budgets, and virements as the year progresses. DSO managers should, for example, make most purchase decisions.

STANDING ORDERS

201.   Revisions to standing orders and financial regulations may be needed. Regulations designed to demonstrate probity but which impose a cost far in excess of the cost of any likely improper behaviour should be carefully scrutinised. The discipline of competition and the need to satisfy the legislation on rate of return and publication of accounts may in some cases be an adequate substitute for a detailed standing order. Procedures to ensure audit trails and occasional sample checks often offer sufficient protection against fraud.

MANAGEMENT INFORMATION

202. Delegated control requires managers to monitor use and income speedily and accurately. This can be done manually, or by using electronic point of sale equipment. Some authorities have more sophisticated systems where point of sale details are automatically passed from the till to a computer system for use in detailed analysis of custom by activity or day of the week, time of day, etc.

203. Costs should also be monitored. Existing accounting systems will often need amendment as they lack commitment accounting, have no interrogation facilities and produce final accounts weeks after the period to which they relate. This involves a major change in the traditional relationship between the DSO and the computer department – the DSO will become the client of the computer department.

204. The overall approach to performance monitoring is summarised at Exhibit 28. Net income/cost is the crucial measure and can be monitored for the whole DSO, for individual contracts, for individual sites when several have been included in the one contract and at cost centre level (squash courts, sports halls, bar/cafeteria etc.) within a site.

Exhibit 28
MONITORING THE PERFORMANCE OF THE DSO
Performance monitoring should be undertaken at a number of levels

LEVEL	RESPONSIBILITY FOR MONITORING	KEY INDICATOR
Entire DSO	Board, Head of DSO	Profit/loss on the statutory account*
Individual contracts	Head of DSO, manager responsible for the contract	Profit/loss on the contract*
Individual sites (e.g. individual pools, leisure centres, golf courses) where more than one site is included in a contract	Manager responsible for the contract, site manager, marketing manager for the site[†]	Profit/loss on the site*
Cost centres within a site (e.g. squash courts, sports hall, bar, cafeteria in a leisure centre)	Site manager, marketing manager for the site[†], cost centre manager	Gross cost, gross income and operating profit/loss on the centre

*   *Taking into account any 'deficit guarantee' or other contractually agreed fees paid by the client*

†   *The site manager and the site marketing manager may be the same person*

205. The budgetary structure for a site should reflect this approach and identify each major income generating centre. Only directly attributable costs should be charged to them. Those which cannot readily be allocated (e.g. receptionist's costs, cleaning costs, energy costs) should be treated as a separate cost centre. The structure should not be over detailed; though expenditure will need to be recorded in full there is little point in having 40 or 50 expenditure sub-heads, half of which contain a few hundred pounds each. A useful, practical structure used by one authority visited is shown in Exhibit 29 (overleaf).

Exhibit 29
A BUDGET STRUCTURE FOR A SPORTS CENTRE
One authority visited used the following approach for expenditure and income centres

Admin.	Ground maintenance	Bar/ Catering*	Premises	Special events*	Recreational activities*
– general – memberships*		– bar trading account – catering trading account	– floral displays – air/heating – general – other fixed plant – water treatments		– sports hall – pool – squash – conditioning room – creche – other admin. – recreational activities

> * *All are expenditure centres. Only those marked with an asterisk are income centres.*
> *Budgets contain only those costs which the assistant manager responsible for the cost centre can control.*
> *The computerised database containing cost and income data can also be searched and analysed using standard subjective heads – employee costs, supplies and services etc.*

206. Usage (i.e. numbers of visitors) and utilisation (i.e. percentage of available time slots which are actually sold) also need to be monitored, to provide an audit check on financial data and to meet any client side management information requirements included in the contract. The data can also be drawn upon in examining bar and catering performance. Other costs – staff, energy, cleaning, repair and maintenance etc. – should also be monitored.

207. Appendix E includes descriptions of some performance indicators which DSO managers can use. DSO managers can also draw on ideas in *Development and operation of leisure centres*, in the Greater London and South Eastern Sports Council's *Measuring performance* and in the Commission's 1988 publication on performance review*. Exhibit 30 describes some ways in which such indicators can be used to manage performance.

Exhibit 30
USING PERFORMANCE INDICATORS TO HELP MANAGE DSO PERFORMANCE
Analyses such as these can help

TYPE OF ANALYSIS	USE
Trend – monitoring profit/loss, income, use, utilisation etc. from day to day, week to week, month to month, year to year.	Changes in performance quickly recognised. Successful initiatives can be identified and copied at other sites. Problems can be identified quickly, investigated and remedied.
Comparisons with similar periods in previous years.	Complements trend analysis allowing managers to take account of seasonal effects e.g. in swimming pool use.
Comparisons with other cost centres or sites.	Helps identify successful initiatives which can be copied elsewhere. Also helps identify cost centres and sites which are under-performing.

* *Performance review in local government - data supplement, HMSO, 1988*

THE BUSINESS PLAN

208. The changes involved cannot be made haphazardly. The DSO needs a business plan which identifies its managerial arrangements and which contracts it expects to bid for. The document should also summarise the marketing plan and proposed staffing arrangements. Other costs and predicted net profit should be given together with an outline of investments to be made. The management and financial information the DSO will use to monitor and manage performance, the changes needed to current arrangements and responsibility for making those changes, with a timetable for their introduction, should also be included (Exhibit 31).

Exhibit 31
THE BUSINESS PLAN
The business plan needs to have a comprehensive coverage

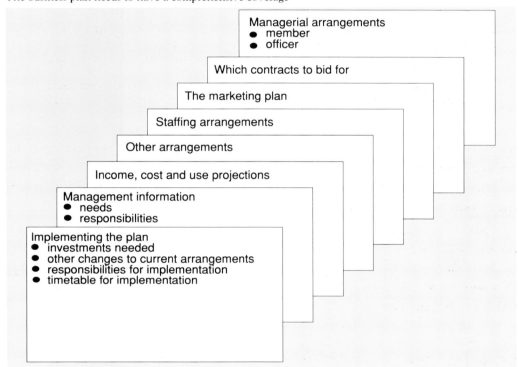

Managerial arrangements
● member
● officer

Which contracts to bid for

The marketing plan

Staffing arrangements

Other arrangements

Income, cost and use projections

Management information
● needs
● responsibilities

Implementing the plan
● investments needed
● other changes to current arrangements
● responsibilities for implementation
● timetable for implementation

209. The plan should be updated at least annually, and more frequently if performance and profit are below expectation. Agreeing this annual update, and receiving the annual statutory report and accounts, should be the major duty of the board or other member body overseeing the DSO.

THE DRY RUN

210. The DSO should establish a contractual relationship with its client as soon as possible so that both can learn from experience before entering the mandatory CCT process. The initial business plan can then be that required for the quasi-contractual relationship and can later be updated to provide the plan for winning work in competition.

211. Together, the measures set out in this chapter and summarised in Exhibit 32 (overleaf) offer DSOs a realistic chance of winning work in competition.

Exhibit 32
PREPARING THE DSO FOR COMPETITION
DSOs should embark now on a programme of preparing for competition

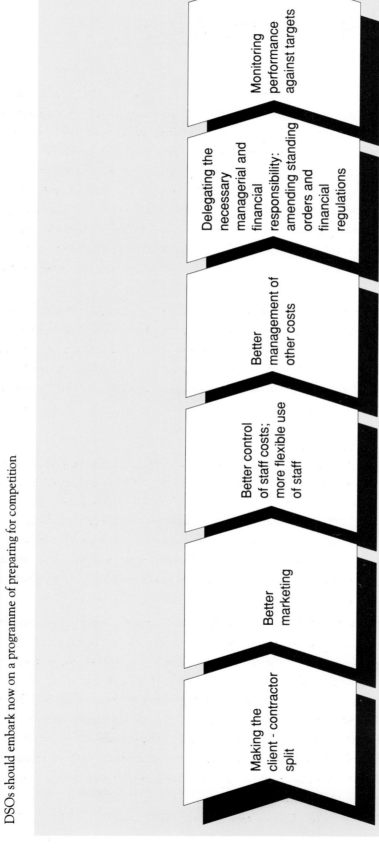

Making the client - contractor split

Better marketing

Better control of staff costs; more flexible use of staff

Better management of other costs

Delegating the necessary managerial and financial responsibility: amending standing orders and financial regulations

Monitoring performance against targets

4. Dual Use

212. The term 'dual use' describes facilities which are reserved exclusively for the use of educational establishments at certain times but are made available for public use at others and have been provided either solely under local education authority (LEA) powers or by the joint exercise of LEA and other (S19) powers. In shire counties the latter normally involves cooperation, often through a joint committee of both bodies, between the county council (as LEA) and the district council (exercising its S19 powers). Similar cooperation, between ILEA and borough councils, is currently found in inner London. In metropolitan districts and outer London joint provision normally involves the simultaneous exercise of LEA powers (usually via the education committee) and of S19 powers (usually via the recreation or leisure committee) by the one authority. Joint provision facilities are usually, though not always, on or adjacent to school sites.

213. Arrangements for community use of sports facilities in schools will, in future, have to be organised within the terms of the Education (No 2) Act 1986 and the Education Reform Act 1988. Major issues which arise are discussed in *Youth and sport – physical education and community recreation – bulletin no 1 – A review and interpretation of recent education legislation* issued by the Sports Council for Wales. Management of dual use facilities will also have to take account of the CCT requirements of the Local Government Act 1988.

RESPONSIBILITY FOR PREMISES

214. Control over the use of school premises outside school hours was passed to the governors of most schools under S42 of the Education (No 2) Act 1986 but subject to direction by the local education authority having regard to the desirability of use by the local community. The Education Reform Act 1988 is now introducing local management and delegated budgeting to schools. Each LEA outside inner London has submitted for approval its own scheme for local management of schools (LMS) within guidelines issued by the Department of Education and Science and Welsh Office; each draft scheme describes the way in which local budgets are to be allocated.

215. Nothing in schemes of local management should, however, restrict LEAs' freedom to issue such directions within the framework of the 1986 Act or maintain existing community provision on school premises*. If LEAs choose they may delegate the management of all staff to the governing body, including staff dealing with public use of sports facilities; alternatively these services can be provided under separate management. In both instances schools will need to be compensated for any extra cost; they should not be forced to subsidise public use from their share of the education budget. Equally, dual use should not over-compensate schools. Inaccurate compensation would undermine the formula basis for allocating budget shares to schools. LEAs can still specify conditions or give guidance to the governing body, for instance on charging and letting policies.

---

* *(para 180, DES Circular 7/88 and para 177, Welsh Office Circular 36/88)*

216. Facilities which are not a part of school premises are not affected by these requirements. Dual use can therefore continue, not only in the form in which the LEA or school makes facilities available to the public without involving a recreation department or a district council but also where there is inter-departmental or inter-authority cooperation. The role of the governors will, however, often be more important and it is essential that LEAs cover community use school sports facilities in their local management schemes.

217. Where the LEA has passed responsibility for community use to governing bodies this may encourage some schools to unlock facilities not now made available to the public, provided the income is expected to more than cover any extra cost. These schools, and the prices they charge, the quality of their facilities and the users they target, will be a further factor in the local sports facility market.

218. The need to ensure that there is no unintended cross subsidy of public use of educational facilities means that the gross and net cost of public use will need to be much more clearly identified than at present. Currently, overall costs are usually allocated between public and educational use on a percentage basis; the actual costs of the two types of use are not calculated. This is unlikely to be sufficient in future.

DUAL USE AND CCT

219. Facilities provided under S53 of the Education Act 1944 (whether or not also provided under S41 of that Act) and whether or not also provided under S19 of the Local Government (Miscellaneous Provisions Act) 1976 are exempt from CCT providing they meet certain minimum conditions on the number of hours educational establishments have had exclusive use of the facilities. Some dual use facilities provided by a joint committee of two or more authorities may also be exempt from CCT under de minimis rules as the de minimis threshold applies to the joint committee and not its 'parent' authorities.

220. Authorities which do not wish to place management of dual use facilities to competition will need to check what powers were and are used in their provision and the number of hours of educational use. The extent to which LEA powers were and are used will then have to be examined. Whether or not the condition that the facility is 'provided' under the relevant powers is satisfied will have to be decided for each facility individually. Simple provision of land by the LEA may not, for example, be enough.

221. The exemption applies when actual use by educational establishments exceeds the minimum, not if availability for educational use is above the threshold or if the public is excluded for the minimum number of hours. Records of use need therefore to be examined carefully; where they are not available, recording systems will have to be introduced as a matter of urgency.

MANAGING DUAL USE FACILITIES

222. Management of most dual use facilities is unlikely to need to go to competition (though there is nothing preventing authorities voluntarily doing so). Cleaning, ground maintenance and catering in such centres is, however, covered by the Local Government Act 1988 and will normally have to be exposed to competition.

223. Many authorities may not wish to put management of dual use facilities to voluntary competition. The management principles described in this handbook should, however still be followed. Dual use management should have a quasi-contractual relationship with the client (whether provision involves co-operation between different departments in the one authority or co-operation between authorities). As with other facilities this involves:

— clearly separating the client and contractor roles;

— giving the dual use operator the freedom to run centres, within the client's policy requirements.

224. Dual use centres can then be managed in the same way as other facilities, using the approaches described in Chapter 3. Centre management will then be able to act in a businesslike way, to increase use and income, within the client's policy guidelines. The arrangements needed for effective management of dual use facilities are summarised at Exhibit 33.

Exhibit 33
MANAGING DUAL USE FACILITIES
Authorities which do not wish to give school governors control of dual use facilities must respond to LMS and CCT by

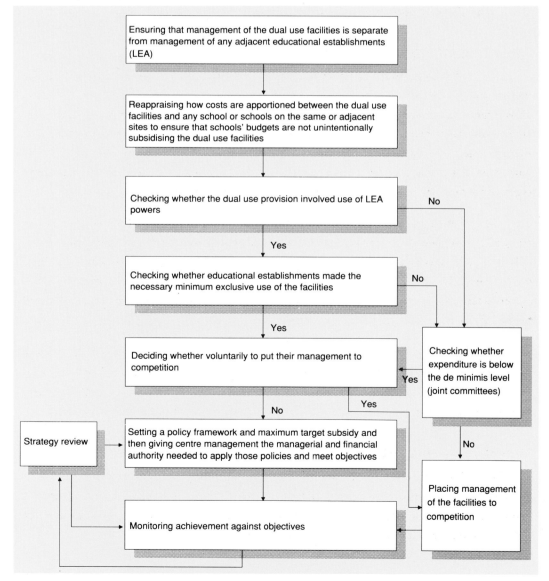

*   *   *

225.   The Local Government Act 1988, the Education Reform Act 1988 and other challenges facing local authorities in their involvement with sport provide an opportunity for them to re-examine what they are trying to achieve and how best to achieve it. During 1990, auditors will be working with authorities in the run up to compulsory competitive tendering to advise them how to get the best out of these opportunities. There will also be the opportunity to draw on the experiences of those authorities which have put sports management to competition earlier than prescribed by the legislation.

Appendix A
AUTHORITIES VISITED

The following authorities were visited during fieldwork:

Babergh District Council

Blackpool Borough Council

Bolton Borough Council

Bournemouth Borough Council

Bracknell Forest District Council

Broadland District Council

Cardiff City Council

Chelmsford Borough Council

Cheltenham Borough Council

Chichester District Council

Chorley Borough Council

Crawley Borough Council

Darlington Borough Council

Doncaster Borough Council

Dudley Borough Council

Exeter City Council

Gedling Borough Council

Great Yarmouth Borough Council

Hambleton District Council

Havering Borough Council

Hinckley and Bosworth Borough Council

Hove Borough Council

Lancaster City Council

Lliw Valley Borough Council

Newark and Sherwood District Council

North Norfolk District Council

North Tyneside Borough Council

Nottinghamshire County Council

Rochford District Council

South Bedfordshire District Council

Surrey Heath Borough Council

Thamesdown Borough Council

Vale of White Horse District Council

Wansbeck District Council

Waverley Borough Council

Westminster City Council

Wokingham District Council

Appendix B
THE CLIENT – CONTRACTOR SPLIT

1. Under CCT a local authority should regard itself principally as a policy maker and employer of contractors; an authority's own DSO may act as contractor but only if the work is won in competition.

2. The need for a clearly defined client role is incontrovertible; where clients should be located within the committee and departmental structure is debatable. There is a range of options. The Audit Commission believes strongly that there should be a clear separation between client and contractor and does not favour approaches in which the two remain within the same department or report to the same committee. At member level, separation is best achieved through separate committees. A number of authorities have achieved this separation for other services by having the DSO report to a board, constituted as a sub-committee, of say, the Policy and Resources Committee. At officer level separation can be achieved through separate departments or through clear definition and division of responsibilities within departments.

3. The main reasons for advocating separation are:

— clients should be concerned with policy, service standards and value for money. Contractors should be concerned with winning contracts and performing to standard and price; the demands of this function are quite different. 'Two-hattedness' could muddle priorities and result in officers and members compromising objectives; for example, the client's specification could be influenced by considerations directed to supporting the in-house contractor and unrelated to the council's overall objectives;

— the in-house contractor is more likely to operate competitively if separate from the client. In many authorities achieving competitiveness will require changes to basic working attitudes, methods, pay and conditions. These changes are more likely to be achieved where the manager can manage in a more businesslike way. In a small authority where there is no separation of client and contractor the post of DSO manager may be too junior to be sufficiently attractive to a high calibre manager;

— it will demonstrate that the authority is serious about giving equal treatment to all contractors – private or in-house. Leaving the in-house contractor in the same department as the client may dissuade contractors from bidding (thus reducing the prospect of improved VFM) and leave the authority open to accusations of anti- competitiveness, whether or not there is substance to the charge;

— it will help authorities put more emphasis on general management skills rather than professional qualifications.

4. The Audit Commission's earlier work on other services affected by CCT has illustrated some of these points; client policies and budgets can be driven by DSO considerations when officers have both responsibilities. Budgets are staffing-led and service levels are not altered as needs change, leading, for example, to over-frequent sweeping, gully emptying and grass cutting and to over maintenance of vehicles.

5. Such considerations easily outweigh the possible disadvantages of a full client-contractor split. Some authorities claim that adverse consequences may be:

— longer lines of communication between client and contractor;

— skill shortages – it may be difficult to split managers between departments where there is only one person at a particular level or if two work together as a good team;

— an overall increase in expenditure in small authorities resulting from two separate operational structures. The Commission has found no evidence so far that separating client and contractor increases staffing requirements substantially.

6. Client side rationalisation, particularly in smaller authorities which already have many chief officers and committees, is an essential part of the preparation for competitive tendering. Fears among some chief officers about loss of position and status can hinder both this process and the introduction of a clean client-contractor split. The nettle must be grasped and authorities should ask whether they need to restructure so that they have a small number of client committees and departments. It may be possible to group functions which require similar skills; for example theatres, museums, art galleries, sport and parks might be grouped in a leisure department.

Appendix C
CLIENT SIDE PERFORMANCE INDICATORS
The following are measures which the authority can use to monitor the effects of its involvement with sport.

SUCCESS IN MEETING POLICY OBJECTIVES

Number of people participating in sport (all facilities)	i.e. Numbers of people of different sexes, ages and social backgrounds (including target groups) taking part regularly in sport, irrespective of whether or not they use local authority provided facilities (defining regularly as, say, at least once a week).
Participation rate (all facilities)	i.e. The above expressed as percentages of the numbers of people in the different groups.

CONTRIBUTION OF FACILITIES PROVIDED BY THE AUTHORITY TO MEETING POLICY OBJECTIVES

Number of people participating in sport (local authority provided facilities)

Participation rate (local authority provided facilities)

EXPENDITURE

Net expenditure by the authority

Net expenditure by the authority per head of population

Net expenditure by the authority per head of population (excluding debt costs)

EXPENDITURE PER PARTICIPANT

Net expenditure by the authority per participant (all facilities – private, voluntary and local authority)

Net expenditure by the authority per participant (all facilities) (excluding debt costs)

Net expenditure by the authority per participant (local authority provided facilities)

Net expenditure (excluding debt costs) by the authority per participant (local authority provided facilities)

CONTRIBUTION WHICH INDIVIDUAL LOCAL AUTHORITY FACILITIES MAKE TO MEETING POLICY OBJECTIVES

No. of participants i.e. no. of people who use the facility:

— more than once a week

— weekly

— once a fortnight
etc.
analysed by age, sex, social group, type of activity.

No. of user visits   i.e. no. of user visits, analysed by age, sex, social group, type of activity.

COST OF THAT CONTRIBUTION

Average subsidy to or net income received per participant	i.e. Cost to or net income received by the authority ÷ no. of participants
Average subsidy to or net income received per participant (excluding debt)	i.e. Cost to or net income received by the authority (excluding debt) ÷ no. of participants
Average subsidy to or net income received by the authority per user visit	i.e. Cost to or net income received by the authority ÷ no. of user visits
Operational subsidy to or income received per user visit	i.e. Net payment to/from contractor ÷ no. of user visits

CONTRIBUTION WHICH SPECIAL ARRANGEMENTS MAKE TO MEETING SOCIAL OBJECTIVES

Number of passport to leisure holders	Possibly further analysed by different target groups (unemployed, retired etc)
Take up rate for passport to leisure (i.e. no. of holders ÷ no. of people entitled to cards)	
No. of user visits to facilities provided by the authority made by passport to leisure holders	Possibly further analysed by individual facility and by target group
No. of such visits as a percentage of total visits	
No. of participants in sports outreach activities	Number of different people who take part in at least one sports outreach activity a week
No. of new participants reached by sports outreach activities	Number of different people who previously took no part in sport but who take part in at least one sports outreach activity a week
Continuation rate	e.g. % of sports outreach participants stilll taking part regularly in sport 12-24 months after leaving a scheme or the end of the scheme.
New participation continuation rate	e.g. % of new sports participants taking part regularly in sport 12-24 months after leaving a scheme or end of the scheme.

COSTS OF SPECIAL ARRANGEMENTS

Expenditure on marketing
and administering passport
to leisure scheme as %
of total expenditure
supporting sport

Expenditure on sports
development and outreach
schemes as % of total
expenditure supporting
sport

Expenditure per
sports outreach
participant

Expenditure per new
sports participant reached
by the outreach programme

Appendix D
JOB DESCRIPTION – A DSO MARKETING MANAGER
1. GENERAL PURPOSE

The marketing manager will be responsible for marketing ABC Centre – market research, strategic and operational marketing, and promotional activities.

2. KEY TASKS

The following will be carried out on an on-going basis:

a. Market research

This will involve:

— identifying who does and does not use the centre, and reasons for their use or non-use;

— splitting the potential and current users into sub- groups by whatever means seem most appropriate;

— a comprehensive review of the services (products) offered by the centre;

— identifying the sub-groups (segments) which appear commercially worth attracting, and the services to offer them, taking into account any constraints set by the client;

— modifying the 'product portfolio' so that it better suits the wants/needs of the 'target groups'. This may involve dropping some products, developing others, and introducing new ones.

b. Strategic marketing

Pricing proposals will be developed by the marketing manager, for agreement by the client as necessary. Consideration will be given to 'loss leaders' and activities which cover marginal costs without generating a contribution to fixed costs. The marketing manager will be encouraged to attract non-sporting events to the centre, where allowed by the client's specification, if these are profitable.

The marketing manager will also be responsible for establishing and promoting a corporate image for the centre.

c. Promotion

Having identified the segments of the market that the centre will try and attract, promotional activities to inform these target markets will be needed. The marketing manager will be responsible for deciding the best way to reach these segments, and the best media to use.

d. Customer care

Liaison with the manager and other staff on presenting products and customer care. Arranging customer care training as necessary.

e. Performance monitoring

The marketing manager will monitor the utilisation of facilities and their profitability, modifying and developing the centre's management information system where necessary. Customer satisfaction and complaint levels will also be monitored.

3. ORGANISATION

It is not currently envisaged that there will be any other staff employed full-time in a marketing role in the centre.

The marketing manager will report directly to the director of the centre, and will form part of the management team.

He/she will hold a marketing budget, part of which may be used to buy in any consultancy support needed to carry out the key tasks.

Appendix E
PERFORMANCE INDICATORS FOR USE BY DSO MANAGERS

Possible indicators include:

ENTIRE DSO AND INDIVIDUAL CONTRACTS

Profit/loss	Gross income (including any 'deficit guarantee' payments from the client) less gross expenditure (including any fees, profit or income shares or other payments to the client).
Operational income	Income (excluding any deficit guarantee income from the client).
Operational expenditure	Expenditure (excluding payments to client).
Operational profit/loss	Operational income less operational expenditure.
Operational recovery rate	(100 X operational income) ÷ operational expenditure

INDIVIDUAL SITES

As for DSO as a whole plus:

Fee income from users	Admission charges from users.
Other operational income	Bar/catering, advertising, shop sales, special events etc.

No. of users

Fee income per user

Other operational income per user

Total operational income per user

Operational expenditure per user

PER SPORTING COST CENTRE

(Sports hall, pool, squash courts etc)

No. of users

% utilisation(dry space)	Percentage of the time available for hire that the space is actually hired. Calculated in badminton court units for sports halls.
Fee income	Admission charges from users.

Fee income per user

Variable expenditure	Costs which depend on how the cost centre is used. Normally staff costs plus those of any equipment leased or purchased by the DSO. Actual energy charges may be included if separately metered and if they can be influenced by the assistant manager responsible for the cost centre (e.g. by switching off lights when no users are present; proper attention to energy saving measures in a pool).
Marginal profit/loss	Operational income less variable expenditure.

BAR/CATERING/SHOP COST CENTRES

Operational income	Income from sales.
Variable cost	Staffing costs, cost of purchases etc.
Marginal profit/loss	Operational income less variable cost.
Operational income per sports user	

SPECIAL EVENTS COST CENTRE(S)

These may be treated as a cost centre, either globally (one cost centre for all events) or individually (one cost centre per event). Indicators are:

Operational income	
Variable cost	Staffing costs, costs of purchases etc. The room used (e.g. a sports hall) may also be treated as a cost, subject to an internal recharge to the cost centre which normally deals with the room.
Marginal profit/loss	Operational income less variable cost.

PREMISES COST CENTRE
Expenditure:

— repairs and maintenance

— energy (if not recharged to other cost centres)

— cleaning

— rates

— ground maintenance

ADMINISTRATIVE COST CENTRE

Costs:

— receptionists' costs

— on site admin

— central recharges

— marketing

— other

Income:

— memberships

— advertising

The exact definitions of these items will vary from DSO to DSO depending on local circumstances. For example some authorities now charge for and/or count spectator admissions; others do not. The important thing is that each DSO has clear local definitions which it can apply consistently to compare performance between contracts and sites, and between cost centres within a site and which it can use to monitor performance over time.

Printed in the United Kingdom for Her Majesty's Stationery Office.
Dd8190708 1/90 C50 0488/2 12521